What the Locusts Had Eaten

The Nikki O'Baire story

by Jennifer Evans

What the Locusts Had Eaten
The Nikki O'Baire story
by Jennifer Evans

Printed in the United States of America

ISBN 978-1-60266-530-9

Scripture taken from the HOLY BIBLE, NEW INTERNATIONAL VERSION Copyright ©1973, 1978, 1984 International Bible Society. Used by permission of Zondervan Bible Publishers.

www.xulonpress.com

In Gratitude

In many ways, this book has been a group effort. The product is a result of months of tedious writing and rewriting from taped and carefully transcribed interviews with Nikki, who relived much of the process with tears. I am thankful to her for baring her soul for the good of those who will read this account.

Every writer should have a mother like Marilyn Brown. Mom has always been my best cheerleader and close confidant. I am grateful to her; she listened with enthusiasm as her excited daughter read aloud the very rough draft of each chapter of this work.

I am also grateful to those who read and critiqued the manuscript when I had done the best I thought I could. Jane Williams, Cynthia Simmons, Rick Thompson, Emily Laminack, Sandy Freeman, Sherilyn Leath and Jenijoy Arrendale each helped tweak it, catching mistakes and making suggestions that brought it to the presentable form you see today. They have been a tremendous editorial team.

Members of the Atlanta Writers Club patiently assisted in polishing my work as I presented it to them for critique and suggestions. My friend and fellow writer Vicki Kastranek coached me in areas where I was weak and led me to resources that finally resulted in the publication of this story. I am in her debt.

None of this would have been possible without my gracious, patient husband, Gary Evans. He has given me space and time for writing, in-house tech support, necessary finances and consistent encouragement to develop the gifts God has trusted to me. His untiring faith in me is a rare and precious gift I will never completely comprehend. I pray I will never take it for granted.

Most of all, thank you, reader, for choosing this book, reading it and passing it on to someone who needs the hope it can bring.

Author's Note

This book is based on the memories of Nikki O'Baire, and has been corroborated by some of those closest to her. All of the events in this narrative actually happened. Most of the dialogue is as she remembers it, but some conversations were filled in to fit the tenor of the events around them. Every character in this book was a real person; a few names have been changed for reasons that will become obvious.

What The Locusts Had Eaten
The Nikki O'Baire Story

I will repay you
for the years the locusts have eaten –
the great locust and the young locust,
the other locusts and the locust swarm –
my great army that I sent among you.
You will have plenty to eat, until you are full,
and you will praise the name of the Lord your God,
who has worked wonders for you;
never again will my people be shamed.

Joel 2:25-26 NIV

Introduction

I turned off the recorder and sat quietly. Nikki choked on her tears as she whispered, "That's what makes me weep. I didn't realize at the time what I was doing to my kids."

She accepted the tissue I offered and wiped the rest of the smeared mascara from her clear blue eyes. Recovering a trace of voice, she said, "No matter how painful it is, I have to tell this story."

For victims who become wounded parents and pass those scars on as hurts in the lives of others around them... For people who look for love in all the wrong places... For those living on the edge and looking over, finding the other side of the precipice empty... For those who have given up on prayer...

Choices made one at a time, when lined end to end, stretch into a life. God never wastes our pain. That is why we wrote this book. Nikki wants you to know there is still hope.

Chapter One

Swarming Creatures

As I lie staring into his sky-blue eyes, sensing his arm around my waist and feeling his breath warm against my neck, I am utterly content. I wonder again at the mercy of God. First adulterous lust, then cohabitation, then marriage, then divorce and now this – all with the same man – only God could make that happen. I wouldn't wish my life on anybody, but I'd go through it all again if it were necessary to get to this place.

Normal is an opinion. You think you are normal until you compare yourself to others. Then you wonder whether you or they are strange. You count your experiences, your family, and your plans for the future as ordinary while you are part of them, but when they have passed, you realize how much was surreal. You reminisce, watching yourself acting as on a stage and wonder whether you have been involved in a comedy or a tragedy. Experience becomes tragic only if it is wasted. That is why I have to tell you my story.

We called our landlady "Aunt Ruth," although she was really no relation to us at all. She had two sons and three daughters. I suppose her husband was away, fighting in the second World War like my father, because he doesn't have a place in my memory. Aunt Ruth's younger brother, Frank, also lived with them. Mama worked swing shifts and could walk to her job from Aunt Ruth's place. I dreaded the nights she had to work, and Frank was the reason.

"Ruth," her voice faded as she descended the two flights of steep stairs to the homeowner's quarters, "Will you look in on the kids later?"

Aunt Ruth must have agreed, because Mama didn't say more. I followed her footfalls through the paneled hallway into the foyer and heard the heavy front door close behind her.

I was about three years old when Frank started making his night visits. I don't know if Aunt Ruth sent him to check on us or why he came initially, but I knew every time he opened the apartment door what I could expect. His lanky five-foot-ten shadow filled the entry for a moment. He came in and clicked the latch behind him. My baby brother, Chuck, was fast asleep on the lower bunk.

"Hi, angel," he whispered as he leaned over my bunk. He stroked my face and hair. I tried to turn away, but he leaned down and breathed words into the ear that was now on top.

"You are so pretty, like a china doll. Let's play a little game, just you and me, okay? Uncle Frank is gonna help you have some fun, see. This game is just our secret, though. You can't tell anybody, 'cause if you do, things will happen... nasty things. We'll get hurt, and we don't want to do that."

Hot tears coursed my cheeks. I couldn't tell Mama because something bad would happen to me. Uncle Frank was a grown up and he knew about stuff that could happen. His broad hands felt cold as he explored my body... under my nightgown, into my panties went his icy fingers.

Every night Mama worked, it was the same. Frank would come, fondle me and enjoy himself while I cried silent tears onto my pillow. In the daylight, he seemed handsome to others with his dark hair and muscular build. He never lacked for female attention, and I suppose those girls thought he was attractive. But I only knew I hated him.

Night work was good from Mama's perspective because it meant she could be home with us most of the day. Waking and climbing from my roost, I walked around the foot of the bed, turned left and passed through the door to find Mama in the kitchen. This morning, she'd been to the grocery store on her way home. She stood behind the small partition that separated the dinette from the cooking area unloading a brown paper sack onto the table. I spied the margarine, our wartime substitute for more expensive butter. A waxy bag hid the mushy snow-white blob.

"Oh, Mama," I pleaded in my best whine, "please let me work the margarine."

She smiled and handed me the bag. I didn't know it was a job; I thought it was a game. I mashed and mashed with my tiny fingers until I could feel the yellow-orange button hidden in the midst of it. I pressed through the bag until the button popped, ever so quietly, with a dull "phup" and bright streaks of gold splashed into the mass. I kneaded the bag until my little hands ached, watching with delight as the oleo took a uniform color. At the end of the process, I passed the prize back to Mama, happy to please her and feeling grown up with my accomplishment.

"Thank you, sweetheart," she said, bending to give my shoulders a squeeze. She took it around the partition to the icebox, which sat against the alley wall.

"Oh look, Nik," she commented, opening the door. "We're almost out of ice. I guess it's time for a delivery."

I giggled and clapped my hands. Mama laughed at my exuberance. I could hardly wait for the iceman to make his weekly rounds, lugging the huge chunk of frozen water up the purgatory stairs in a burlap bag slung over his shoulder. He dripped his way into the kitchen, slid his burden onto the floor and pulled the drawer from underneath the icebox. Depending on the weather, he would either dump the water from the melted coolant into the nearby sink or throw it out the window. Then he'd replace the aluminum-lined drawer and open the upper door to hide his chilly prize.

"There, missy. How do you like that?" he'd say. He made me smile, talking to me, and he always smiled back. I wonder now what he thought of that nosy little curly-topped redhead spying on his every move. Before he left, he always dried the puddle with a rag hooked into his belt.

"See you next week, sister." He'd smile, climb the steps, step through the door and close it behind him.

In the summertime, our routine was a bit different. Chuck and I would sit outside on the front steps. Since the place was one among many row houses on the street, the iceman would stop his truck once and deliver to several homes during that interval. Salivating, we watched him as he grasped the overgrown ice cube with a giant pair of metal tongs. As soon as he was too far away to care, a gaggle of delighted children gathered around the truck, picking up fist-sized chunks of crystal blue icicles that fell from the large blocks. We studied the ground like pecking chickens gathering seed. Every scavenger plunked one frozen hunk into the mouth and grabbed another in each hand.

On Labor Day Weekend, Mama didn't have to work. I watched her pull my overnight case from under the bed. Excited, knowing somewhere else was on the horizon, I ran and knelt between her and the two steps to the apartment door.

"What are you doing, Mama?" I queried as she dusted cobwebs from the suitcase.

"How would you like to visit Grandma?" She didn't look at me, but smiled at the suitcase.

"Oh, boy!" I shouted as I leaped to my feet. My paternal grandparents lived in a row house in another town, about an hour and a half from us. We traveled on a bus. It stopped in an ancient neighborhood with overpowering wooden porches and towering trees that hid the sun. We had to walk several blocks after the bus stopped. I was fascinated by a hawker struggling down the street with a huge pushcart full of fat, red tomatoes, slick yellow onions, shuck corn and peas still in their tough green shells. Women sat on shady porch steps waiting for the afternoon's groceries to come to them. In the distance, I heard someone shouting.

"What's that noise, Mama?" I asked, grasping a fistful of her skirt and pulling closer to her.

"Nothing to fear, baby," she answered, reaching to take my hand. We rounded a corner and saw the source of the shouting. An innovative fellow, thrown into the joblessness of the post-war era, was traveling the streets calling "KNIIIVES sharpened..." For about three cents each, you could take your eight or ten knives to him and wait while he pulled a wheel from his backpack and did the needed work. The next morning, I saw another crier shouting "CLOOOTHES props!" Looking through Grandma's parlor window I could barely see the man, almost hidden beneath a burlap bag filled with ten-foot wooden poles. Each sported a notch carefully carved in the top, which when properly positioned with one end on the ground underneath a line, prevented wet laundry from dragging in the dirt. I watched him through little girl eyes, amused by the sticks protruding from his back. I know now those were hard times, but they offered wonderful memories.

I loved my grandmother: a gentle, petite woman with a thick British accent. When she saw us coming, she flung open the screen door and came down the steps to meet us.

"Welcome, my precious!" She pecked Mama on the cheek as she cuddled me into a warm hug and smacked a wet kiss onto my face.

"Have ye been a good girl?" she queried, eyes smiling.

"Of course, Grandma. The best!" I teased.

"Perfect. I have hot gingerbread for good girls," she assured me, tickling me until I giggled and ushering us into the house. The place always smelled of fresh baking, and her Aunt Jemima cookie jar with its smiling black face and kerchiefed head never disappointed my sweet expectations.

"Guess what I've got for ye," she asked, pouring milk to go with my cookies.

"A surprise?" Oval-eyed, I waited for her answer.

"Ye cannot guess?" she pressed. I bit my lip and squinted, then shook my head.

"Lavender bath soap," she almost whispered. My delighted expression pleased her.

"But first ye have to help me with the laundry," she insisted, trying to be stern. I finished my sweets and followed her to the back yard.

"Bring me the clothes prop, child." I found it leaning beside the back door, for to leave a clothes prop on the ground was to ask for filth or rot that would mean soiled laundry and the expense of a new prop. I balanced the long pole with both hands, careful to avoid gouging the ground with it.

I stood by the empty basket and watched her adjust the thick stick. Then she hung soggy sheets and damp linens on the line.

"Ye can bring the basket," she told me when the heavy things were hung and only underclothes were left. I obeyed, feeling grown up to be trusted with such an adult task. When the last piece was pinned, she repositioned the pole so the laundry waved high in the wind, shiny clean banners celebrating Grandmother's patient work.

"Now," she studied my face as though she would give me a lecture. "Let's go find that lavender soap."

I held the empty basket on top of my head with both hands and pranced up the steps. After dinner when she made my bed with those fresh sheets, I could still feel the breeze and smell the sunshine.

A worn maxim declares "opposites attract." Certainly it was proven true in my grandparents. The old Irishman's frown is fixed firm in my mind. I never sat on my grandfather's knee or gave him a kiss. When I came into the house, he sat still as a stone in his chair and never said a word. I made the mistake only once of surprising him while he was reading. With a sudden jerk of the head, he poured contempt in my direction: "What do *you* want?" was his angry demand with the characteristic furrowed brow. If my dear Grandmother was delicate and sweet, I can only describe him as callused and bitter. While she was an obedient servant, he was a commanding master. Their relationship was one of the few examples of a long-term marriage I saw as a child. It reinforced to my tender subconscious the twisted perspective for which other men had already laid the foundation.

Mama worked swing shifts at RCA, alternating between days and nights. Once in a while she'd bring home components to show us the kinds of things that she worked with on the assembly line. I looked at the strange objects in her hand: a glass tube, a small round metal thing with wires protruding from the ends, a larger square metal box that looked hollow inside...

"What is it for?" I asked.

Chuck pulled the round thing from her hand and bent the wires into legs, squatting to make it walk on the floor.

"These small parts go on a board where someone melts them with a hot tool. Then they go down a conveyor belt – "

"What's that?" I interrupted.

"It's like a long table that keeps on moving so that lots of people can reach the parts to add their piece. Anyway, this board with these little things on it goes down the conveyor belt and other people add other things until it comes out as a machine – "

"What's a machine?"

"You know, like a washing machine."

I knew about those from Grandmother's house. Chuck and I were wide-eyed with her explanation, especially after she told us when everything was assembled, it came out as an electric box that could show people talking and walking around! It sounded more magical than margarine to these five-year-old ears. One day the first such box was delivered to a neighbor. Chuck and I stood at the window as the rest of the neighborhood gathered outside to watch some men take it into the building. We didn't see the people inside the box, but we believed Mama knew just what she was talking about.

Instead of a television, our evening entertainment came from the daily newspaper. One of the features was a bedtime story for children.

"Nikki, bring Chuck and come to the bed," Mama called.

We abandoned our blocks where we'd been building a fort next to the kitchen door and ran to the living room. She was combing her hair, sitting at her vanity adjacent to the bed. I looked out the window that stared into a brick wall next door. Mama was getting ready to go out.

"Did you brush your teeth?"

"No ma'am," I said, turning toward her and fingering the tiny bottles of sweet scent resting in front of the mirror, killing time and wishing for morning. She picked up the darkest blue one and removed the stopper, dabbing the fragrance behind her ear and filling the room with springtime. For a moment, I forgot my dreaded secret.

"Well, do that first." Her eyes were fixed on me. I knew the story wouldn't happen until I obeyed. I pulled Chuck's arm and he followed as fast as his two-year-old waddle would carry him. I fished my toothbrush from its pint jar and handed him his. After I had made a few swipes across my clenched teeth and Chuck had chewed the paste from his bristles, we both had a drink from the jar and I replaced the toothbrushes. Chuck beat me to Mama's side and crawled over her, cuddling into the crook of her right elbow as I snuggled under the other arm. Mama opened to the page with the story and started to read.

"Once upon a time..." There were no pictures, but if I closed my eyes I could see it. Every minute or two, I opened them just to prevent falling asleep and missing part of the story. Chuck was not as diligent. By the time the tale was half told, he was fast asleep, slumped from his original sitting position into a limp, thumb-sucking heap in Mama's lap.

"Okay, sweet girl, time for bed." She leaned over and kissed me on the forehead, gathered Chuck gently in her arms and took him to the bunk. He slept on the bottom, I on the top.

"Mama, do you have to work tonight?" I asked her as I climbed to my roost.

"Yes, baby, but I'll be home by the time you wake up."

I felt tears coming, but Mama kissed me and turned out the light before they trickled across my cheek. I knew I would have a visitor before I saw Mama again.

I learned later in life that one of my cousins had Frank's baby when she was fourteen. Her mother made sure she went away until the child came, and before anyone could talk, it was adopted. I wondered what else had happened in that house since he also had three young nieces living there.

Frank started teaching me at a tender age that men are predators and women are their prey. As life went on, several others would reinforce the lesson.

Chapter Two

Mouthfuls of My Heart

My younger brother, Chuck, grew up thinking our father didn't love him. I don't remember the first time I met my Dad, but I knew he cared about me. He came occasionally and took me home to visit with him and my stepmother at their beach house. He looked like a movie star: auburn hair and bright, dancing blue eyes.

For me, Chuck was always "little brother." He was born when I was three, so as far back as conscious memory can follow, he was in my life. However, for my proud, Irish daddy, Chuck's birth must have been a crushing shock. He found out mother was pregnant by another man during his lengthy overseas tour of duty. Chuck didn't have a father who didn't love him; he had a father he didn't know. After we were adults, Mother told us the truth. That was when I put the pieces together and Chuck began to deal with the baggage in his life from that ugly beginning. Perhaps he was the innocent scapegoat for my father's silent anger about the divorce.

Growing up together, we assumed we were full siblings, and no one ever told us different. I loved being with Chuck, and for the first few years of his life until I started school, we were constantly together. When he got big enough to sit up in the tub, we even had our weekly Saturday night bath together. Mama would fill the basin and toss us a bar of Ivory and a few toys. We'd laugh and play "Catch the Soap" and splash each other. By the time we were done, there was almost as much water on the floor as there was left in the tub. Mama didn't scold us, nor did she seem to mind the mess. During the week, we got washed with a rag every day, but we both loved Saturday nights best of all. Chuck was my precious brother, my buddy and my playmate. I spent my childhood protecting him, but I wasn't really big enough to do it.

Chuck was two when Arthur started coming to the apartment to visit Mama. I know because I wasn't in school yet. Arthur was about five foot ten with a beer belly. He reminded me of a vampire from a scary movie I'd seen: a little strip of slick dark hair on top and nothing on the sides. To this day, I don't know what Mother saw in him. They had grown up in the same town, and although he was older than Mama and ran with a different crowd, they had friends in the same families, so their paths sometimes crossed while they were in school. Perhaps it was loneliness that mitigated her interest. Maybe she feared raising two children on her own, and wanted a father for us.

I suspect she never intended to become pregnant; I have wondered if the relationship coagulated around the coming addition.

Odie was born before Mama and Arthur married in 1949. I remember the event well; I was already a big girl at seven. Aunt Ruth took Chuck and me downstairs when the midwife came.

"If you listen, you might hear that new baby cry!" She created great anticipation and excitement for us about the event. We welcomed the tiny child into our household and became a perfectly normal family. A few years later, Mother and Arthur had another son, Stephen. Then our clan was complete.

I started that September at the neighborhood elementary. We lived in the middle of a block. Walking up the street, crossing and continuing another short distance, I could get to school. By then, Arthur had moved in. He seemed nice enough and our lives were peaceful. Frank had faded into the woodwork and was no longer a problem. Soon, though, our little flat proved far too small for five. We moved back to Moorstown, the place where Mother and Arthur had been raised. We were only there part of a year, then moved to another town. Even though I had to change schools again, I liked this apartment better. It was larger and I had my own bedroom. That would prove to be both an advantage and a disaster.

The house, situated on a hill, sat at ground level on the front side but my bedroom in the back of the building was on the second floor. My room had a single bed instead of bunks and on the wall next to the door a massive chest of drawers stood tall on stubby carved wooden legs. I immediately loved the windows for the light and air they let into the room. There was a huge, stationary solid pane in the center. On either side were smaller panels, opened by a straight metal handle that twisted to free a latch, allowing the entire piece to push to the outside. I soon learned to appreciate this easy hardware for more than just aesthetic reasons.

I'll never forget the first time I came home from school to find five-year-old Chuck sitting in the corner, crying and trembling. I dropped my books on the table and ran to him, putting my arms around his small shoulders.

"What's wrong, Chuck? What happened? Did something scare you? Did somebody hurt you?"

His face was red and swollen and he was still crying too hard to really talk to me. He just put his arms around my neck and pulled me closer to him as sobs kept coming. I held him for a long time. He could tell me later. Before Chuck had a chance to calm down, Arthur appeared in the doorway.

"What do you think you're doing?" He glared at me angrily. He'd been drinking again.

"He was crying," I explained without moving from Chuck's tight embrace.

"Don't you console that little brat!" he slurred as his voice escalated to a shout.

"What did you do to him?" I was starting to see that Chuck's tears were Arthur's fault. He took two uncertain steps toward us, staggering, bracing his broad body against the wall. His stumbling seemed to make him angrier. Grabbing the back of the dinette chair closest to his left arm for support, he bent toward us. I stood slowly, putting myself between my terrified little brother and the drunken man's pointed index finger. I could smell the liquor and feel his hot breath in my face.

"He wet the bed," Arthur growled. "and I spanked him. It is none of your damn business," he hissed.

I was shocked. This big lug had hit my brother for wetting the bed? I glanced at Chuck, now huddled wide-eyed in the corner behind me with his thumb in his mouth. Something maternal wakened in me. Mother was at work, and nobody was gonna hurt Chuck.

"You're drunk!" I said, louder than I really meant to, staring at Arthur. "You hurt him! Look at him. He's scared to death!" I didn't know what to do. Maybe if I brought the facts to his attention, he would see the truth, be sorry, apologize to Chuck and go comfort him. I wasn't prepared for what happened next.

"You little BITCH!"

His right hand hit my cheek so hard I fell to the floor. I screamed as the blow landed, then bit my lip. I would not give him the gratification of child tears.

"Don't you sass me," Arthur growled. "I'll give you a good dose of what he got!"

I stood up while he stared at me. Anything could happen now. I knew I was fast and could run, but I couldn't leave Chuck. My mind raced and we stared at each other. At that moment, the phone rang. Arthur waited for the second ring before staggering to answer it. It was enough of a diversion for me to grab Chuck by the arm, pull him to his feet and run.

31

We were out the front door and down the street before our stepfather could know we'd gone. Four blocks from our home was a small park with a swing set and a slide. I took Chuck there and we played until it was time for Mama to be home.

It was dusk when we crept up the back steps to the kitchen and peeked inside to be sure Mama was there. She stood at the stove with her apron on, stirring something in a big pot. I opened the door and cautiously urged Chuck inside. He ran to Mama and threw his arms around her hips.

"Hi, baby." She bent and kissed him on the top of the head. Then frowning, she turned to me.

"Where have you two been? I was worried when you weren't here. Arthur said you'd run off! Nikki, you know you're supposed to do your homework when you come in from school. Then you can go out to play-"

I cut her off mid-sentence.

"Mama! Arthur hurt Chuck. He hit him because he wet the bed!"

"I know that. He told me he spanked Chuck and that he is teaching him to be a man instead of a baby. Chuck needs to learn not to do that."

"But Mama, he was drunk. He hit him hard and Chuck was sitting in the corner still crying when I got home. And when I asked him about it, he hit me, too. Mama, he knocked me down and called me a bitch!"

"Arthur said you sassed him. You know, Nikki, I have told you not to upset him. He has a nasty temper and it's best to avoid making him mad, especially when he has had a few drinks."

"But Mama -"

"Nikki! Don't 'but Mama' me. From now on, I want you to come home and stay home after school. No more of this taking Chuck and running off. Do you hear me?"

"But what if -"

"Nikki? Did you hear what I said?" She had stopped stirring and was staring at me. I knew I couldn't argue. Maybe Arthur would come to her defense if he heard loud voices. Tears swelled my eyes. Chuck was sitting at the table. I ran to my room, shut the door, lay on my bed and cried and cried. I forgot about supper and no one bothered to remind me. She hadn't heard me. She didn't believe me. Did she not love me any more?

The next morning I woke with the sun. I dressed, gathered my books and went to the kitchen. Dawn offered just enough light that I could find the food to make my lunch. I packed a sandwich and filled my chilled thermos with milk. I was finishing the process when Mama came in and flipped on the light.

"My, you're up early. You missed supper. Did you want some breakfast?" She smiled at me and it was obvious that she'd either forgotten or deliberately chosen to ignore our conversation the previous evening.

"I'll just eat some Cornflakes," I muttered and poured them myself. She set the milk bottle on the table and turned to finish making coffee. When the Cornflakes were gone, I turned up the bowl to finish the last drops of sugary milk. Arthur's heavy footfalls were progressively louder in the hallway. Sweeping my books under my arm, I hurried to Mama, gave her a peck on the cheek and told her I had to get to school early. It was a lie, but she was too preoccupied to ask questions.

For several days after that, life was calm. I came home to find Chuck playing in his room or in the back yard with Odie. The weekend passed without incident; Mama was home and Arthur wasn't drinking as much as usual. But on Monday evening, I got to the corner of the yard and froze in my tracks. I could hear screams coming from the house. I knew it was Chuck, and I could tell he was in serious trouble. I dropped my books in the yard and flew into the house, hardly touching the porch as I leaped to the front door. In a terrible second, I took in the scene. A huge, inebriated beast was beating the life out of a small boy. Chuck lay on the floor. Arthur hovered over him, legs spread in an effort to stay upright, fists clenched and flailing. Chuck's arms and legs were bleeding. Leaping with all my might, I landed on Arthur's left side and wrapped my legs around his bulging middle, knocking him off balance. He stumbled sideways as I pounded his face and head with my small fists.

"Get off him! You animal! I'll kill you. I hate you!" I meant every word, and even found a few that I didn't know I knew. I succeeded in distracting him from Chuck, who pulled himself out of the fray.

"Run, Chuck! Go hide!"

He could hardly walk, but he disappeared from the room. I don't know where he went. Arthur slung me from his belt line, and I hit the floor on my back.

The jolt knocked the wind out of me and when I regained my breath, Arthur had both of my wrists in his left hand, pinned to the floor above my head. He was wearing a sinister grin.

"Now what are you gonna do, little heroine? Who's gonna rescue you?" He put his knee across mine as I attempted to kick him.

"No, no. I could break you in half if I decide to," he sneered. In the meantime, his right hand was moving across my abdomen. I wanted to scream, but I didn't want Chuck to come back; he might be in danger. Arthur reached between my legs, but my dress was in the way. It was caught between my clenched knees. As he loosened his hold to raise my dress, I freed one leg enough to kick hard with my right knee. Perfectly aimed, the punt smacked him right under the chin. Suddenly my arms were loose and he was the one screaming! I rolled free and scrambled out of reach, running to my room. Safely inside, I locked the door and looked for a place to hide. I was too big to get under my low bed, and the closet was a small cabinet with a mirrored door. The only other big furniture was the chest of drawers. I could hear Arthur's drunken obscenities in the hall. He slammed his heavy hip against the door. Then the pounding stopped. I heard jingling. He was fumbling for a key. It was then I rediscovered the window. I opened the latch and peered at the ground, two floors below me. The handle rattled and I could hear Arthur swearing. I had no choice. My heart pounding so hard I could almost see it, I pushed the window open, climbed on the sill, closed my eyes and jumped.

It was easier than I thought, and though my landing was awkward, I soon found my feet and ran. I wasn't sure where to go, but then I thought of Pat. Her house was across the neighborhood, but we went to the same school. She was my best friend, and whenever we were away from home, we were together. Lucky for me, she answered the door when I knocked.

"Nikki! You're a mess! What's wrong?" She let me in and hugged me. Then I cried. I told her what happened and how I'd escaped. She helped me wash my face and gave me some milk and a chocolate chip cookie. Pat thought of a game in which each of us had to make up a taller tale than the last. We told each other stories, and she made me laugh and forget my problems. Everyone should have a best friend like Pat.

Just before dusk, I knew I had to get home. I was glad that Mama usually went into the kitchen door since my schoolbooks were still scattered across the front lawn. I gathered them and found the skeleton key I kept in my wallet, which fit the front as well as my bedroom door. I slipped into my room unheeded and climbed to the center of my bed. I had just opened my history book and picked up a pencil when she knocked.

"Nikki? Are you in there?"

"Yes ma'am." She opened the door and peeked in.

"I didn't see you when I came home. Did you get your homework done?"

"Almost. I just have some History and English to finish for tomorrow. She gave us a lot today." Lying was getting easier.

"Well, you'll have to finish it after supper. Come and eat. And close that window."

Life with Arthur slowly became a recurring nightmare. He beat Chuck multiple times for wetting the bed, and would slap me, hit me with his fists or kick me any time he felt like it for no reason at all. I became adept at launching myself through the window and running. The strange part about his physical abuse was the lack of it toward Odie and Stephen. They were never the objects of his wrath; just Chuck and me.

I can't remember exactly when Mama changed to third shift, but then the nightmare got worse. Not only did Arthur beat us in the daytime, but at night, he started coming into my room. Even when he was drunk, he could use the key, so locking the door didn't help. Clad only in his underwear, he would crawl into my bed and rub his body against mine. I was a sliver of a girl, and as a third grader, was virtually helpless against his advances. I turned away. I curled into a fetal position. I tried freeing myself to run, but when he caught me, he threw me onto the bed and threatened me. He pulled my clothes off. I suppose he could never get me still long enough to really penetrate, but it wasn't because he didn't try. I kicked and bit, I cried and screamed, but the boys were too young to understand what was happening, and Arthur just snorted a laugh. He probably considered me a daunting challenge.

Night after night this scene was repeated with slight variations. I tried to tell Mama, but she didn't believe me. She'd just get angry.

"Nikki, you don't need to make up stories to try to turn me against Arthur! There is no need for you to be jealous of my time with him. He is a good man. You know he'd never do those things you are telling me. Of course, he drinks some. Just stay away from him. I don't know where you get this stuff!"

I gave up on her rescuing me. I realized much later in life that Mother was like so many women in love with a scoundrel: trusting him, protecting him, and doing her best to believe in him against all evidence to the contrary. Sometimes, love isn't blind; she just closes her eyes.

One night I had an idea. Anger and desperation gave me the adrenaline rush I needed. As the sun set, I pushed and tugged at my giant chest of drawers until I slid the edge of it across the door facing. Later that night, I heard the keys rattle and the doorknob turn, but then I only heard Arthur swear. He couldn't get in. That night, I slept well. The next morning, though, Mother tried to open the door to wake me up.

"Nikki? Nikki! NIKKI!" She was angry by the time I stirred enough to answer.

"What do you have against this door? Move it right now!"

I had a miserable five minutes in my half-alert state trying to shove the chest without the aid of fight or flight chemistry coursing through my veins. Finally she entered, and her face glared her discontent.

"Young lady! You are not to block this door again. What if there had been a fire?"

"I'd go through the window," I responded calmly.

"Don't get smart with me! Now get ready for school. And hurry up! You're already running late because of your little shenanigans."

I dressed without trying to explain. I could almost see Arthur's smug smile as he draped himself over a cup of coffee at the kitchen table.

I didn't listen to Mama. I practiced shoving the antique and learned to wake at dawn to move it back before she came. One night, though, I didn't get it in place fast enough. Arthur changed his schedule and came in while I was finishing my homework. The two youngest boys were asleep, but Chuck was brushing his teeth. Arthur was in his underwear, very drunk, standing in my doorway when Chuck came through the hall on his way to the bathroom.

"Goodnight, sir," he said, stopping to look at the half naked man.

"Go to bed, brat," Arthur snarled, half under his breath.

"Sir?" Chuck said, not having heard the command. The six-year-old didn't move, waiting for clarification. Arthur pushed himself away from the door facing and lunged in Chuck's direction. Now my brother knew what to do, and he ran in his footed pajamas toward his bedroom door, but it was too late. In three steps, Arthur caught him and jerked him up by one arm. The boy screamed with pain and I saw tears on his face. Suddenly his pajamas were wet and so was Arthur's leg.

"Why, you little bastard!"

"No!" I screamed just as the old man slapped my defenseless brother across the face. He was cussing and shaking Chuck. I ran and kicked him hard in the back of his right knee, which obediently buckled under his weight. He dropped Chuck, who sat in a wet, crumpled heap on the floor. I hoped he would crawl to his room and go under his bed where I'd taught him to hide. Arthur shouted some other obscenity in his direction and turned on me. I ran to my room and slammed the door, but there was no time to move the dresser. There was no time for anything. I grabbed the window latch, slung the pane as far back as the hinges would reach and flung myself into the darkness. I didn't know where I would land, but it couldn't possibly be worse than the alternative.

That night, I ran to Pat's, but instead of knocking on the front door, I went to her bedroom window.

"Pat! Pat!" I shouted in a whisper. I was in luck. She was in her room.

"Nikki! What are you doing here? What happened? What time is it, anyway?"

"Pat, come with me. I've got to run away!"

"Again? Nikki, you know they'll only pick us up and call your Mom to get us like they always do." She was right; we'd tried it before and not succeeded.

"But this time, we'll go a long ways. If we start now, they won't even know we're gone until morning. Pat, if I stay there, I'm gonna kill him."

"Wow, that bad, huh?"

"Yeah, worse," I assured her. Pat sneaked through the back door and joined me in the yard. She put her arm around my shoulders, and we started walking. It was a cool, windless, pitch-black early autumn night. I think she came with me to try to talk me out of it, because neither of us thought of bringing money, extra clothes or even a blanket. We just started walking. We headed for the main highway, and since no one had ever taken us that direction, we had no idea where we were going. We walked and walked and talked for hours. Finally, we saw a dim glow on the horizon.

"We're getting somewhere," I said.

"Yeah, but where?" Pat wondered.

We soon found ourselves in a town square of sorts, but the place looked deserted. A lone streetlight leaned over a fire hydrant on one corner.

"Look over there," Pat whispered, as though anyone were around to hear, or to care if they did.

"What is it?" I asked her, but she shrugged her shoulders. We ventured closer.

"I think it used to be a dance pavilion," I decided. The pillars lay askew on the ground with the conical roof intact on top of them.

"We could crawl underneath and sleep," I offered.

"Ooh... what if there's a snake in there?" Pat hated snakes.

"I'd rather face a poisonous snake than go back to live with Arthur!" I reminded her.

"Well, okay, but you go first." I shoved away some scattered splinters and scooted under the collapsed shelter.

"Hey, Pat - it's not bad under here. You can't see anything, but the roof is high enough that you can sit up!" Momentarily, she joined me, giggling.

"We could probably make a house out of this and no one would ever find us!"

"I don't know where we are, but at least we have a roof over our heads. I think I'm gonna try to sleep." I lay on my side and Pat curled up with her back against mine. We were cold, now that we'd stopped walking, but were too tired to care. I folded my arm under my head and soon fell into an exhausted sleep.

Late the next morning a bird landed somewhere near the opening we'd crawled under and chirped. I awoke with a start, frightened and disoriented for a moment. Then I remembered: Pat was here and Arthur wasn't. That was the good part. On the other side of the coin were all the facts: we were miles from anything we knew, had not a penny between us and were both ravenously hungry. We took turns rubbing our eyes and yawning for several minutes before either of us spoke. Pat's whisper broke the silence.

"I need to *go*," she said, peering out the hole we'd crawled through.

"If you can do it in here, nobody will see," I told her.

She struggled her panties far enough below her knees to avoid wetting them, held up her skirt and pulled herself up to a squat. When she was finished, she manned the entrance and I took my turn in our makeshift outhouse.

"I wish I wasn't hungry. Then I don't think I'd be sorry we did this."

"Pat, I can't go back there. He is a beast. We have to find somewhere to live."

"I vote we find breakfast first." She stuck her head through the hold in our shelter to spy out the land.

"I don't see anybody. Let's get out of here." She slid into the daylight and I followed her. The sun felt good, but it didn't fill our stomachs.

"Let's wander around and see if there's food, like milk or something, on somebody's doorstep," I suggested.

"Nikki! You'd steal food?" She looked at me with wide eyes.

"It wouldn't really be stealing if we only took one bottle because we are hungry," I assured her. "It's not like we plan to make a living at it, you know."

"Yeah, I guess you're right."

We headed for the corner with the streetlight. It led to an alley where people were lying on the sidewalk. Two filthy men shared a dirty blanket, fast asleep. An equally disheveled woman squatted on the other side of the alley, digging through a trash can. Pungent odors of rotting food spilled into the clean street, and I suddenly felt nauseated.

"Why are those people here?" I murmured as I hurried away from the smell.

"What? Slow down, I'm too hungry to run," Pat complained as I slowed my pace.

"Did you see that woman digging in the garbage?"

"Yeah, she was probably hungry, too," she noted, tossing me a sideways glance.

"Eat garbage? I don't think I will ever get that hungry!"

We turned a corner and found ourselves in a neighborhood of single family homes. It wasn't as hard for me to be hungry as it was for Pat. Arthur actually rationed our food, mine and Chuck's. Odie and Stephen always got whatever they wanted, but not us....

"You go around behind that side and look on the back steps, and I'll take this side," I instructed. "The first one to find a bottle of milk, whistle."

She reluctantly agreed, and we started our quest. Ten minutes later we met at the corner on the other end of the street.

"No luck," she said. "It's too late in the morning. All the women have put it in their iceboxes by now." I knew she was right.

"Well, let's just go back to town and go to a restaurant and see if they will give us anything."

"Beg?" There was that wide-eyed stare again. She was starting to get on my nerves.

"Do you have a better idea?" My temper was becoming vocal.

"Okay, don't get mad."

We walked the three blocks back to town, but as luck would have it, a police car pulled up beside us just as we crossed the main street. I wanted to run, but I knew it wouldn't do any good. Besides, I was too weak to go very far. The officer rolled down his window.

"Good morning, ladies," he started. "You look a little lost. Could I help you find someone?"

"Uh, yessir." I was thinking fast. "We are here visiting my grandmother, and she sent us to get some sugar. We got kind of turned around since it was a new place and all. Could you tell us where the grocery store is?" I thought it was plausible, but he wasn't buying it.

"Didn't your grandma tell you?"

"Yessir, but I forgot."

"What is your grandmother's name? Maybe I know her and could call and ask her for you."

I didn't think fast enough, so the officer parked his car and got out.

"I don't think you'd be here visiting relatives when school has already started. Why don't you both get in the car, and we'll go down to the station and sort this out."

Pat was staring at her feet. I knew she was about to cry, and I felt like it, too. We were caught again.

He asked us where we were from and then he took us back to the police department in our town where Mama was waiting for us. He left us facing her and retreated into the adjoining room. She was livid.

"What in heaven's name do you think you are doing?" she screamed. "Just how many times are we gonna go through this before you decide to behave yourself? I am getting sick and tired of searching for you all over town!" Her face was red and her make-up was smeared. She kept screaming and yelling, stomping and kicking like a crazed animal, but I had stopped listening. Voices in my head were screaming back at her, at the policemen, at all the adults in my life: *How dare you stand there and scream at me when that monster beats me and attacks me and hardly lets me eat! Nobody cares what happens to me. All you want to do is send me to detention. I could die and nobody would even care...*

Chapter Three

Locust in a Cricket Suit

In my hometown, the Police Department sponsored a program for young people: *The Police Athletic League*. They did more than just athletics. On Saturdays, they aired *The Pal Show* on a local radio station. When auditions were held, I was chosen as a regular soloist. Each Saturday, I walked to the broadcasting office to do the live performance.

Someone involved in the Police Athletic League had connections with the U.S.O. In the mid-50s, patriotism was high and military bases in this country were full and active. I started working with *The Pal Show* when I was twelve. At fourteen, looking like eighteen, I was invited to join the U.S.O. team. Mother signed her permission for me to be involved. We performed for the local military bases in their canteens. I soloed with *Canadian Sunset*, *Love Is a Many-Splendored Thing* and other popular songs of the day. Music was in transition between big band sound and rock and roll, so we had a wide repertoire.

One night after we'd finished a show with a "Roaring 20s" theme, Mother and I were backstage preparing to board the bus when a man approached. He introduced himself, and Mother spoke for her and me.

"I really enjoyed your show, young lady," he told me. "You have tremendous talent. In fact, it's because of you that I'm here."

"Oh?" Mother said. "And just what business would you have with my daughter?" she asked him with characteristic frankness.

"We are getting ready to do a musical on Broadway, and Nikki would be perfect for the part," he announced. "I would like to set up the details so she could audition for it."

I'm sure my face was glowing with excitement. I wondered what Mother would say, but she didn't disappoint me. She and the man talked more while I went inside to change into street clothes. Evidently his answers met her approval, because when I came out, she was smiling and shaking his hand.

"Nikki, is this something you think you'd like to do?"

"Could I, Mom? It would be a dream!" I was on my way!

In the process of planning for that audition, another opportunity arose. A small local record company was looking for talented teenagers, and they asked me to do some recording with them. They required a photo shoot in costume and make-up at a studio in downtown North Camden. We lived on the east side, and as it turned out, Mother couldn't go with me the day the pictures were to be taken. Late in the afternoon, I climbed on a bus and ventured alone into the big city. The appointment was for 7:00, and the trip took an hour or more. By the time I arrived, it was dark.

The receptionist led me to a studio where another woman told me she would do my make-up. Several people were talking in the room when I arrived, but soon the others left and only one young man and the make-up lady stayed with me.

"You know, I think this is the wrong color base and blush for a redhead," she said. "Why didn't somebody tell me what color pallet to plan on? It's going to take me about twenty minutes to find what I need. Honey, are you in a hurry?" She smiled at me.

"I don't think so," I told her, not sure how to respond.

"Okay, then. I'm sorry for the delay. Just wait here, will you? I'll be back as soon as I can." She gathered her brushes and colors and hurried out, closing the heavy door behind her.

Pictures of various recording artists lined the walls. Soft carpet muffled footfalls on the floor. I stood to study the portrait nearest where I'd been sitting.

"Who is this lady?" I asked the man. I wondered absently if my picture would someday hang in this room.

"I'm not sure. She was before my time," he answered, standing behind me. I made two steps to look at another glamour shot when I heard his voice getting closer.

"Why don't we have a little fun before we go out there and do this photo? You'll have a natural blush in your cheek," he said, lowering his voice a little. I turned to face him.

"What are you talking about?" I asked, not at all comfortable with the way he was looking at me.

"You can't be that stupid," he said. "What do you think I am, an idiot?" He narrowed his eyes a little, and Arthur's face flashed through my mind.

"You don't understand. I'm just fourteen. I don't know what you're talking about." I tried to tell him the truth, but he wouldn't listen.

"Yeah. Right. Sure you are! If you're so young, I'll show you how it's done."

"I think I already know, and I don't need any more lessons. Certainly not from you!"

He was close enough to touch me now, and he did. His hands were on my breasts and he was pressing me against the wall just under the picture I'd been admiring. I pushed at him with my hands, but he pulled them to my sides and pinned them there with his elbows, going back to explore my chest and waistline. His face was against mine, his mouth on my cheek, my neck... In desperation I gathered my wits and stomped his left foot as hard as I could. His grip loosened and I slapped his face. That was enough of a deterrent to allow me space, and I ran. He didn't move; I suppose his foot wouldn't cooperate. I yanked the door open and raced down the hall to the elevator. I didn't know how many floors it was to the reception desk, but I was in a hurry to get there. I called Mother and within the hour, she came for me. I told her what happened through streaming tears.

"I guess I can't let you come down here alone," she commented.

The pictures never happened. However, two weeks later, a man and his secretary were to pick me up at home and take me to the studio for the recording session. When he arrived, his associate wasn't with him. He parked on the street at an angle from our living room window. It was dusk when he arrived. I kissed Mother on the cheek and assured her I'd be fine, then went with the agent to his car, now shaded by the growing night. Before we even left the curb, he reached over, pulled me into his arms and tried to kiss me!

"Leave me alone!" I screamed. I wriggled from his grasp and slung the door open. I went back in the house and told Mother I wasn't going. I didn't tell her the real reason; I just told her I felt sick. It wasn't entirely a lie; my soul ached. Was this how all men acted?

Several days later, the record company called, determined to finish the work they'd begun with me. Mother took me to the studio and I did the recording. The local stations played it for a while, but that was as far as it went.

By the time I was fourteen, I had learned not only to push my dresser across the locked door and bolt through the open window, but also to fight back. Arthur never tired of the struggle. He must have had masochistic inclinations because the more I fought, the more he seemed to enjoy it. A month before my fifteenth birthday, something happened that put an end to his advances.

Pat was with me on this particularly frigid Saturday walking home after the PAL Show. Gray clouds threatened to pile more snow atop the half-melted gravelly slush mounded into dirty little hills on the sidewalk. Bitter wind tore at our jackets and wrapped our skirts tight around our hips and boots, making it hard to walk. We pulled scarves close around our faces and didn't attempt conversation.

Traffic buzzed by us on the busy street to my left, but I didn't pay much attention to it until a brown '49 Mercury pulled up and its engine slowed to an idle. We stopped walking as the driver reached across to the passenger window and lowered it.

"Hey, you girls need a lift?" Gorgeous blue eyes smiled from beneath a healthy mop of brown hair. With his high cheekbones, square jaw and sharp nose, he looked like an actor. It took only a split second for me to know he was a dream... and he had a car! But I was not eager to ride with him. He was a man, and I hadn't known many nice ones.

"No! We don't need a lift," I responded with brave determination, and resumed walking. Pat followed without speaking. He wasn't taking no for an answer... the car inched along beside us.

"Oh, come on. I'll take you. I promise you I'm not a bad guy. I'm not a wolf. If you want, I'll drop you off at your house or at your corner or whatever, and I'll be on my way. But you just look so cold out there...."

I knew he was being a wolf, but Pat turned to me, her eyes pleading. The fellow couldn't hear her, but I'm sure he knew she was softening.

"Come on, Nikki! Let's go!" she begged.

"No! I am not getting in the car with him," I told her.

"Come on," she insisted. "We can sit in the back seat...."

I saw her face; we were both freezing. Now I was softening. I turned back to the blue-eyed canine.

"Well, look," I started, as seriously as I dared, "if we sit in the back seat and you won't lock the doors...."

"No, I won't lock the doors," he promised.

"And we can just sit back there, I can show you where we live, you drop us off and that will be all?"

"Consider it done, ladies." His smile convinced me that he was genuine, so we climbed in. The warm car soon relaxed us and we untied our scarves. My hair fell across my shoulders and I caught the driver's gaze in the mirror. I lowered my eyes.

"I'm Bert," he said. "And what are your names?"

"I'm Nikki and this is Pat," I answered, now feeling more comfortable. He smiled again into the mirror. I pretended not to notice.

"So what are you two young ladies doing later?" he wanted to know as we drove along.

"Go right here." I ignored him. He turned the corner and repeated the question.

"We're busy," I lied.

"Nikki, we're not..." Pat intoned softly.

"Yes we are!" I mouthed a shout to her in a whisper. He must have seen me in the mirror.

"Ah, come on... I know where there's a really fun dance. Why don't you let me take you girls to the dance?"

"No, I don't think so," I answered quickly.

Poor Pat; her eyes were whining in my direction. We hardly ever had the chance to do something fun, and he had offered to take both of us. We'd be together; what could happen?

We pulled up to the corner where I'd asked him to let us out. He was the perfect gentleman. Not to mention those blue puppy-dog eyes.... *Well, why not?*

"I'll ask my mom, then," I told him. After all, I owed Pat something for her loyal friendship.

Mama was sitting in the living room when I walked in.

"How did it go?" she asked, looking up from the newspaper.

"Oh, fine. It was really cold coming home. Looks like it might snow again."

"I know; I've been watching the sky all morning and hoping you'd get here before it started. Why don't you go in the kitchen and put the kettle on and we'll have some tea?"

I was glad she was in a good mood. I laid my coat across a chair and pulled the scarf through one arm, then headed for the kitchen. As the kettle whistled, Mama joined me. I set the steaming teapot on the table and went to the cabinet to get cups. Now was as good a time as any; she'd brought the paper and spread it on the table.

"Mama, I met this nice boy and he wants to take me to a dance in Beverly. It's going to be at the firehouse." She heard me, and now I had her attention. Somehow I'd hoped she would just keep reading and say yes.

"How do you know him?" she queried. I had to think fast.

"He's been coming to the radio station to work with the show," I told her. "His name is Bert. The radio station manager likes him, and he seems really nice. He comes most Saturdays. Anyway, Pat and I both want to go, and Bert said he'd take us both." I only partly lied....

"This 'Bert' has a car? How old is he?"

"Not very old, Mama. It would be rude for me to ask him, don't you think? He gave Pat and me a ride to the corner today, and he is a very safe driver. Went real slow."

"Does he live here?"

"Oh, yeah – over near the high school." I didn't know, but I was hoping it was true.

"Well, I suppose if you and Pat go together, it will be all right. Call Pat and let me talk to her mother."

I dialed the phone, and Pat answered. I told her Mom wanted to talk to her mother. Each of us gave up the phone. I waited while our mothers came to agreement.

"All right. I will tell Nikki the same thing," I heard her say before she hung up.

"You be home by 9:30 and not one minute later. Do you understand?"

"Yes ma'am!" I quickly gulped my tea and excused myself before she could ask any more questions. We were going to the dance!

"Oh, Nikki," she called before I made it to my room.

"Yes ma'am?" I stopped and she came from the kitchen.

"When you get home, bring Bert in. I want to meet him."

"Sure, Mama," I answered, relieved. If he'd impressed me, I wasn't worried about what Mama would think of him.

Pat and I dressed in our cutest circle skirts and did our best to look grown up. Bert had told us he'd meet us at 6:00 on the corner where he dropped us off, and sure enough – he was right on time. The station was filled with teenagers. Pat stood against the wall and watched us dance...and dance...and dance.

"You're not dancing with my friend," I complained to him after the third one.

"Well, if you must know, I really didn't want to bring your friend, but since you wouldn't come without her, I didn't have a choice. I really wanted to be with you because you're absolutely gorgeous! I just love redheads."

He made me blush and I smiled at the compliment. After that, I didn't insist he dance with Pat. He was very sweet, and I enjoyed every sappy line he fed me.

After the dance, he dropped us both off at my house. When I started to get out, he touched my arm.

"Would it be all right if I called you?"

"Sure," I said, and scribbled my number at the bottom of an old grocery list I'd tucked in my handbag.

"Mama wants to meet you," I told him as I passed him the slip of paper. Just as I'd expected, Mom approved of my new beau.

That was February. I turned fifteen in March. He kept calling; we went to the movies, to dances, to dinner. One night after a date, Arthur was on the front porch when I came home. We saw him from the car.

"Let's wait a minute before we get out," I suggested.

"Why? I'd kind of like to meet your Dad."

"He's *not* my dad!" I retorted, a little more vehemently than I intended.

"Hold it. Wait a second...Okay, maybe we need to talk about him."

He looked at me tenderly and started the car. I watched as Arthur stamped out the cigarette he'd been smoking and staggered into the house. Maybe he wouldn't wait up for me.

Bert drove around the corner and down the street to the playground Chuck and I had frequented. Tears welled up in my eyes and spilled in silent rivulets over my cheeks. Bert pulled me close to him and wiped my face with a handkerchief. How could he understand? He was a preacher's kid. How could I tell him? What would he think of me?

"I'm listening," he said softly. Then he was quiet.

I told him the whole story that no one else except Pat had ever heard. When I finished, he reached over and took me in his arms. He held me close and didn't say anything for a few moments. Then he pushed me gently back and took my chin in his right hand, gazing into my tear-stained eyes.

"That will stop," he assured me. "I'll fix it." His face was serious and stern. I knew he meant it.

I don't know what he said to my stepfather, nor exactly when it happened, but from that point on Arthur never laid another hand on me. It was a relief to sleep through the night, to have the luxury of peaceful, uninterrupted dreams. Bert was my savior.

By spring, Bert had asked me to marry him and I was quite ready for a legitimate way to leave home. I loved the idea of being a bride and a homemaker, and Bert seemed the man of my dreams. However, he asked me to stop singing with the U.S.O. and requested that I not do the Broadway audition. I will never forget the conversation I had with Mother about my choice.

"Nikki, you had better be sure you want to do your life this way, because once you've made this decision, your opportunities for a musical career are over. Do you understand that?" She was not scolding, but telling me the truth.

"Yes, Mother, I realize that. But Bert doesn't want me doing this stuff any more. He wants me to stay home: cooking, taking care of the house and being a wife. That is the more important thing, isn't it?" I responded. My impressions so far of a music career had been less than positive.

"Being a wife and probably a mother is important, but I just want you to realize what you're giving up. You've got a few things lined up here that could possibly give you what most people want: a career, money, popularity. Those things go a long way, too. You just have to decide what *you* want." She was right. Had it not been for the hell I lived in at home,

I might have made a different decision. I thought I loved Bert, but I *knew* I hated Arthur.

June 29, 1957, was our wedding day. I was fifteen, he was nineteen. Mom did the best she could on a limited budget; we planned a beautiful wedding and a reception with lots of family and friends. My dress was a traditional lovely white satin gown, complete with train and veil. Irene, a neighborhood friend, was my maid of honor. I had asked Pat, but she couldn't afford to buy a special dress and our family was doing good to pay for mine. Irene's gown was pale lilac, and the three bridesmaids wore summer yellow. Steve was Bert's closest friend and agreed to be his best man. Three other teens stood as groomsmen, looking spit-shined and uncomfortable in their tight patent leather shoes and ill-fitting rented tuxedos.

The First Assembly of God Church was a massive gray stone building that seated about four hundred. Under the rectangular sanctuary, a full basement housed offices and classrooms. The church's spire climbed into the sky and punctuated the air with a cross. Bert's family had attended First Assembly for many years, and his late father had once been the pastor. I wondered how much Bert thought about his dad that day and whether he missed him. My fiancé was a typical preacher's kid, the kind that makes members of the congregation shake their heads and whisper behind their hands. He stayed within the expectations of the church for the sake of his family, but never applied its teachings to his own personal life. He was a "Christian" only in the sense that he affiliated with them.

The wedding was scheduled for one o'clock. It was twelve forty-five when Mother, Irene and I arrived. It was a blistering hot day, and I had a feeling I was already starting to melt. Though the car windows were open, we were happy to step onto the walk in front of the church. At that moment, Mrs. Harrison, a long-time friend of Bert's family, clattered down the stairs in her spike heels and hurried in my direction.

"My dear, you simply cannot come in yet! There's been a small problem..." Before she could finish Pastor Maxwell joined us and addressed Mother.

"It seems the groom has forgotten the ring! I was wondering... since it is twenty-five miles back to his house and the time is getting late, if we might borrow your ring for the ceremony? Nikki would wear it only to the house for the reception and could exchange it there for hers."

"Absolutely not!" Mother almost shouted in the pastor's face. "She will be married with her *own* ring. I will not allow my daughter to exchange rings outside the ceremony. It wouldn't be proper." And that was that!

So at Mrs. Harrison's insistence, Irene and I climbed back into the sweltering Chevy to wait while Bert and Steve made more than an hour's round trip to his home to get my ring. All the windows and doors in the church were open, and I could see my guests waving paper fans and sponging their glistening faces with dainty white handkerchiefs.

It is a good thing I didn't know what was happening to the other half of the nuptial couple. Only later did I hear the whole story from my frazzled groom.

Steve chauffeured on the way to get the ring, but Bert insisted on driving the return trip. They were speeding, doing about sixty in a forty-five mile zone to get back in some measure of good time when Bert heard a siren and saw a red light flashing in the rear-view mirror.

"Uh oh," he mumbled. "We're sunk."

The boys pulled over. The officer stopped behind them and stepped to the window.

"You got a license, kid?" he demanded.

"Sure, officer. I've got two of them today!" Bert grinned, then turned to wink at Steve.

"Don't get smart with me. You were doing fifteen miles over the limit."

"Yeah, I know. I was in a hurry."

"Boy! You better watch your tongue, or I'll have you to jail!" He was scowling. "Are you gonna show me that license?"

"Officer," Steve started.

"You shut up. I ain't talkin' to you."

Bert fished out his license and handed it to the policeman.

"I was going to my wedding," Bert offered.

"Well, if that ain't handy. Why didn't you leave a little sooner if it was so important?" the older man sneered.

By now Bert was getting irritated with the needless delay.

"I forgot something important, and had to go back home for it," he tried to explain, but there was more edge in his voice than he intended.

"Okay, that's it. You, Mr. Smarty Pants, are going to the station. And you," he said, glaring at Steve, "can come along for the ride! You can drive the car, and Mr. Smarty will ride with me."

"Oh, man!" Bert climbed out of the drivers' seat and the officer pushed him against the car, yanked his arms behind him and snapped handcuffs on his wrists. He opened the door of the squad car and shoved Bert into the seat. It was a ten minute ride to the station. Bert wished he could see his watch, and he wondered what the people at the church were thinking. Then he considered his fate. *Could they put me in jail for speeding? Would they prevent me from getting married? Will Nikki ever forgive me?*

They pulled up behind a low brick building. The officer jerked Bert by the arm and led him inside. Steve parked and followed them.

"What have we here?" asked a senior officer who was sitting behind a pile of paperwork at an over-sized desk. "You are certainly the best-dressed criminals I ever saw!"

"Sir, we are on the way to my wedding," Bert answered, still wearing the handcuffs.

"My gosh, son. Did you rob a bank on the way, or what?" the man almost smiled.

"They were speeding, sir," the aggravated policeman interjected.

"I suppose so, if the story is true. Son, do you have any proof of where you were going?"

Steve stepped up. "Yes sir," he said, and pulled the black box from his pocket. "Bert forgot the ring, and we had to drive 25 miles to his house to get it.

We were on the way back to the church. The wedding was supposed to start an hour ago, sir."

"Good heavens, Jenkins! Give the boy a break! This is his wedding day, and he has the ring here... just let them go." Turning to Bert, he added, "I was a nervous groom once myself, son. You'll have enough hassles in life; you don't need one today." A key turned in the cuffs, and Bert reached to rub his sore left arm.

"Thank you, officer," Bert said, turning to Steve. "Let's hope they're still there," he said quietly as they moved toward the door.

"Wait!" The captain's voice boomed through the hallway. The boys stopped in their tracks and turned to face him. "Jenkins here feels so bad about detaining you, he's gonna give you an escort to the church. What's the address?"

Bert smiled and explained where they were going. It turned out to be the fastest trip he'd ever made in a car, following red flashing lights.

For over an hour, Irene and I had been sitting in the Chevy with the doors flung wide, then pacing the sidewalk, then standing under a shade tree in the yard. He would come back. I knew he would....

At two-thirty, I heard a siren and saw flashing lights. My heart raced. Something had happened to Bert! He was hurt – no, there was his car right behind the police car. I was confused, but happy to know he was back. Their car pulled behind the church, and I was finally allowed to go in. I don't know what I looked like by then, but Bert didn't seem to care. He stood at the altar to receive me, and the ceremony was over in a matter of minutes. I was a wife!

In retrospect, it was ridiculous for Mother to demand that Bert fetch my ring. We were going to his house anyway for the reception. One hour would have rescued the entire day, but we couldn't have known it at the time.

His family owned several lots on one section of acreage which they had divided and given to each of their children. The property behind Bert's family home was a lovely garden, complete with ancient shade trees, flowering shrubs, a trimmed lawn and a romantic grape arbor. It was the ideal setting for our reception. When we arrived from the church, several family friends had already been busy setting up a buffet between the trees and putting finishing touches on the decorations. Lavender and yellow crepe paper danced in the gentle afternoon breeze. Tables were dressed in soft, linen cloths to match the lemonade in the punchbowl. Like ladies in waiting, tiny china plates surrounded a carefully tiered wedding cake. Lavender ribbons graced the chairs at the head table. Someone had the forethought to lay a long cloth runner from the back door of the house to our seating area so my dress wouldn't become stained. I smiled at my handsome groom. Everything was perfect.

"Let's take some pictures first," someone suggested. I didn't see the person, but assumed it was the photographer. A groomsman shuffled me across the cloth trail to an archway at the grape arbor. Irene grabbed my train, and I stopped while she bundled it to lay across my sleeve. Just then I realized I hadn't been to the bathroom since before I got in the car. It was after four o'clock, and I was ready.

"Wait," I said to my maid of honor. "Let me go inside first." Irene saw my face and understood my desperation.

"Okay. I'll tell them you'll be out in a minute."

"Better make that five by the time I get through all this and then put it all back!" I started to laugh and thought the better of it. I turned and hurried into the house. The bathroom was upstairs. I climbed as quickly as I dared in my heels, stopped on the landing to rearrange the dress across my arm, and paused to look through the picture window. The scene below was idyllic. I couldn't ask for a better memory.

As I suspected, the hose, garters, layers of petticoats and dress took me about five minutes to rearrange. I washed my hands, opened the door and made my way back to the landing. But the scene that had been the epitome of serenity only moments before had now literally dissolved into utter chaos. A summer cloudburst had turned the crepe paper into wads of dripping color. Soggy women slogged through the puddles, soaking their summer sandals as they tried in vain to rescue delicate pastries and carefully garnished casseroles. A huge roast swam in its platter, now pink with brothy rain. My regal cake had surrendered under the first deluge, the top layer sliding from its double foundation and slouching like a drunken woman across the delicate china plates. Someone had covered her with an extra tablecloth, and two men were now hoisting the table to carry the fallen body into the house.

I stood, paralyzed with disbelief. Had anyone ever had such a wedding day? I should have known it was an omen.

Chapter Four

Being Devoured

After the ceremony, we spent two nights on our honeymoon and then moved in with his family. My husband worked for Weyerhaeuser. It was a forty-hour-a-week job, and good money for a nineteen year old in 1957. Bert was from the "old school"; the man works and brings home the paycheck while his wife stays home, cleans the house, takes care of the children and prepares the meals. His father had been a Pentecostal preacher, and although Bert had never accepted faith as a part of his own life, he grew up with black and white, hard and fast rules: you don't listen to music, you don't drink, you don't dance, you don't...you don't....you don't....

Although his parents were together for his entire childhood, he never saw affection demonstrated between them. Bert was a product of all that, and while he was a doting boyfriend, he became a less vulnerable husband. We were both children when we married. Had I been more mature, I am sure our relationship would have been better.

I don't think I was pregnant before we married, but it didn't take long after the wedding because nine months later, our son was born. Bert adored little Emory, but didn't take an active role in his life. He was a faithful provider – a good father in that way – but hadn't a clue about showing affection, playing and pretending or even exercising discipline. That was my job, and I loved it. Although Bert was not tender, he could be passionate; by the time I was nineteen, I had three children: Em, Chuck, and Linda. I was in my element as a mother. Both grandmas lived within walking distance (Mother and Arthur had divorced and she and Chuck lived nearby), so I was never far from help or advice!

Linda's birth is a story in itself. The week after Christmas, we were invited to a New Year's Eve party. I looked like I was having triplets, and had not been out of the house to do anything fun for several weeks. This would give me an opportunity for adult conversation with friends I hadn't seen in a while and a chance to get away from the house. Needless to say, I was excited about the invitation. Bert gave me money for a new dress, and I found a stunning royal blue acetate with accordion pleats all the way around. It was a dream of a maternity dress, and even though I looked like Omar the Tentmaker when I put it on, I bought it.

During the holidays, our washing machine died. So on the afternoon of New Year's Eve, Bert and I climbed in the truck, tucked the children between us and put the dirty clothes in the back to go to the laundromat. While I was loading the washing machines, I had a strange, gassy feeling. Not pain, not cramps, but a distinct bubbly feeling in the area of my lower back. I didn't relate it to my pregnancy since there was no pain. I finished washing, drying and folding the laundry while Bert watched the kids. We reloaded the truck and went home to get ready for the party.

I went to get my dress from the closet. My first cramp hit. *Oh, man... this can't happen now! I ain't gonna do this. I'm going to a party.* So I put the cramp on "ignore" and stepped into the bathtub. More occasional cramps, but I was determined not to notice. I climbed from the tub and dried off. I had just wrapped my towel around me to go to the dressing table when I found myself standing in a puddle. My water had broken. *Well, this is good timing,* I thought as I called Bert. It was 8:00 p.m.

He opened the door and looked at me. "I've got a surprise for you," I said.

"What?" he said, still staring at my face.

"Look down," I answered, following his gaze to the floor.

"Uh oh. I guess we're not going to the party!"

"Yeah, I guess we're not," I said, not sure whether to be happy or sad.

After I got dressed, packed my suitcase and called Bert's mother to stay with the kids, more time had elapsed. My pains were three minutes apart, and the hospital was a half-hour away. It was almost 10:00, and I was dilating fast. We made it to the hospital and they took me straight to the delivery room. Linda was our New Year's baby, born at 12:02 on January 1, 1961.

Although we missed our party, we had an even better celebration: we were the winners of the local "Baby Derby." Annually, the town merchants gave gifts to the family whose baby was the first born that year. When Linda made her debut, they showered her with infant clothes, furniture, gift certificates for baby food, and many other surprises. Not only was she the Derby winner, she was also the first New Year baby ever born in that hospital, which had been open only about six months. Her name is still on a bronze plaque somewhere in their offices.

Early in 1962, I learned I was pregnant again. Bert's salary was already stretched almost to its limit. We could not afford another child! I was angry and frustrated, confused and ashamed. After several days, I became resigned to the idea and began to prepare for another member to join the family. However, at eight weeks, I miscarried. Guilt devastated me. Had I caused the baby's death by my anger? Was I being punished because I didn't want the child? I cried and became withdrawn and sullen. The miscarriage was harder because Bert was totally unsympathetic. I know now that his stern macho exterior protected a terrified young man. He didn't know how to help, and couldn't admit his weakness to the one for whom he was supposed to be strong.

For months, the guilt ate at me. Then I heard about a new drug that could prevent pregnancy! It was a pill; totally painless, virtually effortless and almost guaranteed. The doctor only had to suggest it to me; I was ready for a solution.

It was *almost* guaranteed. I found out I was pregnant just before my 22nd birthday. Although we still couldn't afford it, and the news was a total shock, I refused to be pessimistic. I was determined to carry this child and be happy about it. I somehow felt I was being given a second chance, and I would not jeopardize this one!

During each of my other pregnancies, morning sickness had been an all-day affair for months. With this baby, it was different. I felt healthy and didn't have any nausea! I was delighted to be pregnant, and my sullen demeanor dissolved into joy.

There was only one problem. From the time I found out about the baby, I started having a nightmare. Every night it was the same horrid scene that woke me sweating, panting, weeping and overcome with fear. In the dream, I was at home alone in the house, crying. Outside, a strange woman was pacing, looking in the windows. As she circled the house, she grew bigger and bigger and bigger. Finally she was so huge that only part of her arm would fit through the window. I can still see that arm reaching out to strangle me - pinning me against the wall, her fingernails missing my neck by only inches... Over and over again the dream came until I began to dread going to bed. I would go upstairs, sit on the side of the bed, and realize I couldn't lay down. Some nights I tried to sleep in the lounge chair in the living room. The woman tormented me as soon as I drifted off. I paced the floor to stay awake, and I became exhausted. The baby was growing and the pregnancy was going well, but the stress on my body was taking its toll.

On November 27th, I went into labor, but there were complications. For hours I struggled, but the baby wasn't moving. She was riding high, under my rib cage, where she had been for most of the pregnancy. I had done this three times already; it shouldn't be so hard! The doctor ordered an x-ray to find out what the problem was, but he couldn't see anything. After some time, the baby's heart rate started dropping. I was becoming delusional, convulsive...

Bert told me later the doctor called him in a panic.

"You need to get over here," the physician told him. "We're losing her, and we have to do an emergency caesarian section. We can't even wait for you to come sign the papers. Will you give us permission?"

"You do what you've gotta do. You just take care of her!" He hung up the phone, called a neighbor to watch the kids, and came to the hospital. By the time he arrived, I was already in surgery.

What medical technology couldn't find at that time was a foot-long tumor. It was flat, like a sausage, and was encased in a gelatin-like capsule. It had grown on the right ovary, downward toward the pelvis, across the cervix, and in so doing had pushed the uterus up. My uterus was sitting on this "shelf" with the baby growing inside. The x-rays were going through the gel as though it were a glass of water; the tumor was invisible until they cut me open to deliver my daughter.

After Shelley was safely in the world, the doctor took a frozen section of the specimen and sent it to the lab. Within fifteen minutes, they knew I had cancer. Science has since documented that the early birth control pills were the cause of many kinds of cancer in women. The next morning at 4:00 a.m., the doctor called Bert in for a private conference.

"I am glad to say your tiny daughter is well. However, the news is not as good about your wife."

"What's the problem, doctor?" Bert knew I hadn't died; he was there when I came into the recovery room.

"The tumor that was obstructing the baby's birth is an encapsulated carcinoma. Bert, your wife has cancer."

"Oh my God..."

"We don't know enough about this kind of tumor. Usually it is found only in middle-aged women."

"So why did it have to be my wife?" I am sure his face was expressionless, but his heart was shattered.

"We don't know why these things happen, but we need your permission to do a complete hysterectomy because we need to get out as many of the hormone-producing glands as possible. Then we're going to sit down and discuss post-operative treatments to see what we can do."

"Will she be all right?"

"I must honestly tell you we don't know."

Shelley was only a few hours old when they broke the news to me. Bert and the doctor came in at six a.m. I opened my eyes just enough to recognize them.

"What are you two doing here so early?" I croaked in a groggy voice.

"Well," the kind doctor started, "we wanted to talk to you."

I listened, becoming gradually more coherent with the seriousness of the conversation. Finally he finished. He was waiting for my response.

"Am I going to live or am I gonna die?" I had to know.

The doctor looked me right in the eye.

"I don't know," he answered.

"I know!" I was fully awake now. "I'm gonna out-live you!"

He smiled at my Irish stubbornness.

"You don't get it. I have four children at home I have to raise," I insisted, "and I *will* raise them!"

"Well, if you keep that attitude, you've got a fightin' chance!" He smiled again, but this time it was less paternal. Bert didn't speak; he just came to the bedside and took my hand.

For a day and a half, I nursed my precious Shelley. She was perfect, and I was delighted to have her in the family. Then, just before the surgery, a nurse came to my room.

"I'm sorry, but I have to take the baby now."

"Why? Where are you going to take her?" I was distraught.

"My dear, your little one is going home, but Mommy has to be in the hospital a while longer. You won't be able to nurse her after the surgery. She is going to be bottle-fed from now on. Don't worry; your husband's niece has agreed to help with her at home until you are able to be released."

Tears flowed down my cheeks and my throat ached. I watched as the nurse carried my baby away. Through the shiny steel doors they disappeared. Now my arms were empty and my heart felt that way, too. I wondered if I would ever see my baby or my family again.

Two days after the delivery I had a complete hysterectomy. At that time, x-ray treatment was the best they could do for follow up with cancer patients. For about two weeks, they also gave me some experimental drugs that were just coming on the market. The x-ray therapy went on five days a week for about two months. The treatments left threadlike red scars all over my hips and buttocks, but I recovered. Scars are proof that something has been sacrificed in order to preserve life. I am proud of mine.

Because Bert's father had been a minister, most of the people in that congregation knew us. During my stay in the hospital, many of the members came to visit. They prayed with me and tried to encourage me. It was my first brush with religion. I could tell these people loved me, and it felt good. Maybe it was their influence, or perhaps God was really trying to get my attention, because while I was in the hospital, I had a vision. It was a starless black night, darker than usual after the 11:00 "lights out." I was lying on my back in the bed in my private room. Through the window, a single moonbeam was reflecting off the wall at my feet. As I lay there staring into the darkness, it seemed that a human form appeared: a head, shoulders and arms in a robe. I couldn't see the face, but it was such a vivid vision that I crawled to the base of the bed to get a closer look. I kept blinking my eyes to be sure I wasn't imagining this... two hands seemed to extend to me out of a mist, as though they were under water. I felt deeply loved and at peace. I lay there with my face close to the foot of the bed for an eternal two or three minutes, then the image dissipated and was gone. The next morning, I didn't tell anyone. I couldn't rationalize my experience, so I dismissed it. I thought it was my imagination, but I couldn't forget the love I had felt. Had God sent an angel to assure me I would be okay?

I was allowed to go home by ambulance for Christmas to be with my family, and then returned to the hospital the same way. Shortly after the holiday, I caught a viral infection in the hospital. I could hear the nurses talking, but most of the time I was delirious. I remember being put into a bathtub filled with ice and having more ice poured on me to bring the fever down. Even in my weakened physical state, I am sure my screams could be heard throughout the entire hospital. It was the most horrible experience of my medical history, but it worked. Finally I was strong enough to go home, but was still bedfast. For two more months, I went back and forth to the hospital daily for treatments.

Bert's niece, Helen, was my angel of mercy in those days. Each of Bert's three sisters owned a parcel of the acreage that had formerly belonged to their father. Eleanor's back yard joined ours, so Helen could easily get home or stay over if needed. She not only watched after my little ones, but also took tender care of me in my fragile condition. She was my light in a dark place. She tried to create a stressless space around me, conducive to healing, but Bert didn't help.

"You just need to get out of that bed and start being a mother again. What are you doing? Why are you just laying around like this?" Bert had his tender side well hidden under a hard veneer.

"You leave her alone!" Helen scolded. "Can't you see she is as weak as a kitten? You try going through cancer and all those x-rays. You try having a baby, for heaven's sake! She will come closer to getting well if you help her instead of ridiculing her!"

Helen was right, but Bert didn't change. He grew less patient and more contemptuous with every week I was bedridden.

I had confidence I could recover. I had done it before, but Bert hadn't known me then.

When I was thirteen, I babysat for a woman who lived in our neighborhood. The first time I went to work for her, I was disgusted. Dirty dishes cluttered the kitchen and overflowed the table onto the floor. The toilet was spattered with yellow spots and long, dark hairs clung to the damp sink. Dirt crusted the linoleum like wax. Soiled clothing filled the entire dwelling with the stale stench of sweat. I had never seen a house so vile. I was hesitant to sit anywhere. As soon as the mother left, I opened every window in the house. Some evenings, it got chilly before she got home, but I preferred the cold to the smell.

One day I came home from school and went straight to the bathroom. I lost everything: breakfast, lunch, and more. I was pale and weak, so Mama put me to bed. Overnight I got worse. Not even water would stay down. The next morning, my skin had a deathly yellow-brown cast. I couldn't get out of bed. Mama was terrified. She had no idea what was wrong with me, but she knew that my tiny body couldn't take much dehydration, so she struggled me to the car and got me to the emergency room.

"Is there any place your daughter could have drunk dirty water?"

"I don't think so..." Mama was puzzled.

"Has she been around someone who had hepatitis?" the doctor persisted.

"Oh my Lord! Is that what this is?" Mama's eyes grew wide and her voice found its panic pitch.

"Yes. I need to hospitalize her right away." And he did. I was there for over a month, and still in bed for several weeks after I got home. Mama figured out where I got the sickness, and she forbade me to go back there. One day not long after I'd recovered, the same woman showed up at our front door. Mama opened it and I heard her shouting.

"You have the audacity to come up here and ask Nikki to baby-sit? If you don't get away from my house, I'm gonna hurt you. You get away from here. Don't you ever come back to this house again!" Mama hadn't even let her set foot in the door. She could be a bear if she believed one of her cubs was threatened.

So after that bout with hepatitis, I was no stranger to bedrest. I was determined to get well, but Bert couldn't know that. He had watched his father die, and perhaps buried emotions surfaced when I was unable to snap out of my illness. For whatever reason, he made my life even harder. I needed more support than he was able to give. In addition to his emotional withdrawal and often overt verbal hostility, I had my own fear: would the "monster" come back? Was the nightmare of cancer actually over?

Early in our marriage, Bert and I lived in the house with his mother and another couple who were relatives. This other couple were very active in a small religious sect. He always talked about his church activities. Unlike the Christians who had visited me at the hospital, this fellow was less than genuine in his faith.

After I came home from the hospital, I felt his eyes on me whenever Bert was otherwise occupied. Even after we moved into our own place, he continued his pursuit. One day he leaned over my shoulder while I was peeling some vegetables at the sink.

"Feeling better, are we?" he breathed on my neck. "I'm glad to see that. I've been thinking about you." I turned to face him and backed up.

"What do you mean by that?" I asked him, the knife still in my right hand.

"Oh - praying for you, of course," he quickly added. "I have noticed that Bert is not very kind to you and I just wanted to say you have my pity."

"Thanks, but I don't need it." I was getting tired of his game.

"Look, if you need to chat, just call me sometime. I can come over and offer you a listening ear and some well-deserved sympathy. Poor baby, all you've been through. We all love you so much. I know you've been really sick..."

He was trying my patience. I knew what he wanted, and all of his religious talk was just a thin white-wash. Whenever they visited and he could corner me, he carried on this kind of dialogue in spite of my cold rebuff.

Even when I finally could function at a slow pace, my body had changed forever, and hormones were taking their toll. I was trying to be Mom to three toddlers and a newborn and to be kind to a relentlessly critical husband and meet his needs. Being married had not provided the solace I'd anticipated. Demands, implications and accusations added emotional pressure. And now, I had another parasite waiting to devour me. It was too much. Finally, I broke.

Chapter Five

Stripped to the Roots

It would be easy enough to turn the gas on. I'd close the windows and lock myself in the kitchen. It was a Friday, and Mama had the children for the afternoon. I was supposed to be resting.

I'll be resting, all right: resting permanently! I wonder if anyone will miss me. If I can't please Bert, and can't convince him to trust me... if I can't take care of the children without help and I can't seem to get my strength back, what good am I to anyone? This other guy keeps trying to interfere in my marriage, and he has done a pretty good job of undermining Bert's confidence in me.. Curse him! Before he started all his crap, I thought I could pull out of this. Now I don't even feel like trying any more. Maybe Bert will find a good woman to finish raising my kids.

My thinking spiraled down from there. By the time I'd closed all the windows in the house, I was convinced I was doing the right thing. Everyone would be better off without me. I was just in the way:

a disgrace and a drain on the family. I carefully blew out the pilot lights and turned on the gas. It would be painless and fail-proof.

I was in a stupor, close to sleep with my head on the kitchen table when Mother came to the front door. Somewhere far away I could hear child noises. The doorknob twisted. I didn't move. Maybe they would go away and let me rest. But it didn't happen. Mother had a key, and she used it.

"It smells like gas in here! Oh my - NIKKI! Linda - get the others out in the yard and stay there!" I heard all this but didn't move. I didn't care. I just wanted to die. I heard windows being unlocked and shoved open. I heard the *clack clack* of Mother's heels on the tile floor as she scurried to the kitchen and turned off the gas. Then I felt her hands on me, shaking me and lifting my head.

"Nikki! Nikki - what happened? Nikki, why did you do this?" She knelt and I raised my head and opened my eyes. "Oh, thank God! Baby..." She pulled my head to her shoulder and held me tight, sobbing. I was too weak to cry. I wasn't sure whether to be grateful or angry that my plans had been interrupted.

Mother insisted I drink several glasses of water. She helped me to the bathroom and washed my face, then got me into bed.

"I'm going to call Bert," she announced when I was safely tucked in. That is all I remember until hours later when voices in my room awakened me. Mother and Bert were in the midst of an escalating argument when I woke up.

"You get her some help," Mother was demanding. "A person doesn't try to kill herself if nothing's wrong!" Then they saw I was awake. Bert came to the bed.

"Why, Nikki? I've done all I know to do, and you pull this! I am not sure what to do with you any more."

"Get out!" Mother sneered. "She doesn't need your accusations. I'll call the doctor." She had good intentions, but before she got to the phone, the parasite appeared in the doorway.

"Yes, call a doctor," he said. He told her to have the doctor call his church's hospital in D.C. "They deal with this kind of problem, and I know they'd be good to her there." He looked at me tenderly. I turned away in disgust. Mother came to the bedside, sat down and took my hand.

"Baby," she said, "we're gonna find you some help. You will come through this. Your family needs you. Will you let us get you into a hospital?"

My eyes were closed, but hot tears streamed down my face. "Whatever you think, Mama. I've had it. I can't take any more. I don't care what happens to me; you just decide."

For months after that, memories blur together. White walls of a hospital float through my mind. The smell of chlorine bleach, faces of white-capped people pulling me up to pour a pill into my mouth and chase it with a sip of water... Tied by my arms into IV bottles, pulled from bed to gurney and shifted back into bed after daily shock treatments...My sanity was a threadbare rag poorly draped over a cold, naked soul. A few times, I tried to run away, but security never let me get far. I am not sure where I thought I could go anyway.

Mother and Bert came to see me a few times. In less sedated moments, I could enjoy visitors. However, while I was hospitalized, Bert filed for divorce. It wasn't a total surprise; he'd been threatening since the week I'd come home from the hospital after the cancer treatments. My emptiness couldn't have gotten much bigger at that point anyway.

Months of shock treatments, sedatives and therapy finally mended my coat of sanity enough to convince the staff I could function in the real world. I don't know how long I was out of circulation: maybe four months, maybe eight... It seemed like forever.

The children were waiting for me at Mother's. We all lived together in a one-bedroom apartment for a few weeks. Mother got me a job at RCA where she was still employed. She was on night shift and I worked days, so one of us was always there with the kids. But the living space soon became impossible. The apartment was downtown, and there was not a good place for little ones to play. It was unfair for young children to be cooped up like chickens all the time.

"Why don't you call Aunt Ruth?" Mama suggested one afternoon as she prepared for work. "I'll bet if you could provide support for the kids, she would be happy to board them there for a while until you get on your feet."

The idea sounded workable. Her house had a big yard, and it was close enough to the school that the kids could walk. I called her that evening and made the arrangements Mother had suggested. It worked well for me: the kids had a place to live and play and a healthy diet. I will never know, however, what it did to them. Frank was no longer living there; in fact, he'd moved out of state. But I've wondered in retrospect if there are shadows of that time still haunting my now-adult children. I will never know how much my decisions may have cost them.

During the time I was married to Bert, Mama started dating a short, wiry Italian man named Tony. He'd moved into her place, and even came with her once to the hospital to visit me, but by the time I got out, they had stopped seeing each other. After the children moved to Aunt Ruth's, Tony came again to visit Mother. They went out a few times and it soon became a regular event. One night, though, I learned who the man really was.

It was very late. Since I had to work the next morning, I was already in bed when a furious knocking interrupted my relaxation. I grabbed my robe and went to answer. What could the emergency be? My heart pounded as I half expected a policeman with bad news that something had happened to Mother. I peered through the peephole in the door. It was Tony.

"Oh, just a minute," I said, fumbling with the chain that secured the lock. I opened it just enough to talk with him.

"Is something wrong?" I queried, wondering what brought him here so late.

"No, no. Your mother and I are planning to go out after she gets off tonight," he slurred his words enough to betray his level of intoxication. "Can I come in?"

I wasn't sure how to respond at first, but looking at the clock, I knew Mother would be home within the hour.

"Okay," I said, and opened the door. "There's some coffee left in the pot if you want to heat it," I encouraged, thinking it couldn't hurt. "If you'll excuse me, I am going back to bed. I've got to work in the morning." He made some acknowledgement of my departure and sank into the couch. I returned to my room, closed the door and turned out the light. Dropping my robe to the floor, I climbed into bed. No sooner had I turned to face the wall than I heard the door open. I didn't have time to roll over before Tony was on me! He was small (not much bigger than me), but he was a man, and he was strong. He held me down and I felt his body violate mine. Pure brutality: I couldn't wiggle from under him, I couldn't move. He pinned his forearm across my face so that I couldn't even scream. The whole vile act only took him minutes, and when he was finished, he stood up, zipped his clothes, walked out and closed the door like nothing had happened. I jumped up and locked the door, then climbed back into bed and wept hot silent tears, waiting for Mother.

An eternal half-hour passed before I heard her come in. To my horrified amazement, I heard her greet Tony! He had waited for her. I wasn't going to let this pass. She was going to know, and tonight.

"Mother!" I called loudly through the locked door, "You need to come in here. I need to talk to you."

"Nikki, Tony and I are going out, dear. We won't be long..."

"*Mother! You need to come in here now and talk to me!*"

She mumbled something I didn't understand through the locked door, but I wasn't about to open it with him still out there. "Mother!" I called. "Mother?" No answer. I heard the lock turn in the front door. They were gone.

The next morning she was asleep when I went to work. I knew it would do no good to wake her; she'd be incoherent until after coffee, and I didn't have time to sober her and discuss the matter, or I'd be late. That afternoon, she was gone when I got back. But that night, I waited up for her.

"We've got to talk," I said when she came in the door. My voice was crisp, and she knew I was angry.

"What? You're mad because I went out with Tony after work? We just had a few drinks and some conversation. Now what could be wrong with that?"

"No, Mother. I don't even care what you do with that man. He's a beast. Mother, he raped me!"

"He what? Nikki! I'll not have you talking like that about the man I am going to marry. You're hallucinating, dear. Probably a relapse of some drug they gave you at the hospital. Tony told me you were asleep when he came, and that you'd gone back to bed after letting him in. He was asleep on the couch when I arrived. Raped you? Don't be ridiculous."

"Mother - he did! You never believe me. You didn't believe me about Arthur, either. You are determined to find the lowest scum of the earth to marry. How can you believe that creep over your own daughter?"

Now there was fire in her eyes. She lifted her hand to strike me, but then caught herself.

"I won't bother to hit you. That would just lower me to your level. You little liar. I know your game. You are jealous of any man that takes my focus off you. It's always been that way. I'd have thought you'd outgrown it by now. Why do you insist on being so selfish? Can't I have a life?"

I'd heard enough. By now, the accusations had escalated into screams. Tears came in spite of my determination not to break down.

"You're impossible. I hate you and all your trashy men!" I ran to the bedroom, slammed the door and locked it.

For the next week, we didn't speak. It wasn't really necessary since we were keeping opposite schedules. Exactly seven days after our fight, I came home to find her closet empty and a note on the kitchen table:

Tony and I have gone to Florida to get married. I changed the apartment rent and the utilities into your name.

It wasn't signed, but I knew who it was from. It was fine with me. They belonged together: one who hurts, the other who betrays. Perhaps they would get what was coming to them.

Months went by, and my bitter soul festered. *How can she say she loves me and do this stuff? How can she let these kinds of things go on? Why didn't she believe me? Why does she love that horrible man instead of me?*

While I was critical of Mother's boyfriends, I was no better at choosing men. Bored in the evenings and sorry for myself, I had developed the habit of barhopping even before Mother left. I didn't consider myself promiscuous, but I did have several different romances in succession over the span of a couple of years. Finally, Bert called to ask if we could patch things up. We moved into a high-rise apartment and brought the children home. It seemed at first as if things were better, and we were going to make it. Then he started spending time with a woman he'd been seeing while we were separated. I confronted him.

"We can't make a family work if you're gonna do this. Do you think your behavior will lead to a happy marriage?"

He wouldn't budge, so we separated again. The divorce was still in place. For a while, we tried to work things out. He moved in with another woman and they had a child together: Tommy. After the baby was born, Bert left her and came back to the kids and me. He became the maintenance manager in the building where we lived, and soon I learned that he was carrying on with a woman who lived in the building! Enough was enough. He'd been unfaithful in more ways than one, more than once. There was no foundation left on which to rebuild our marriage.

Not long after Bert and I had first divorced, Mother and I had moved into a two-bedroom place and taken a roommate, Janet, to help with the rent. Like me, she was in her mid-twenties and was part of the hippie generation. She was dating a free-spirited Dutchman. We'd stayed in touch, so after Bert and I gave up our efforts, she called me.

"Yannis has this friend you should meet," she told me. I was ready for a new adventure, but this one would prove to be a ride in the fast lane heading straight for hell.

Chapter Six

Famine

In the mid-sixties, youth culture took a radical turn, and I was right in the center of it. We believed in feeling good, looking casual and being free. At least, we thought we were free. Yannis' friend, John, was sweet and kind. He loved to talk, seemed genuinely interested in me and gave me the attention I'd been craving. He was everything Bert was not.

Six of us went to the Woodstock Rock Festival together. My red hair was waist-length, and I wore long crinkle-wear skirts and thin, loose-fitting blouses. I don't know when we started smoking pot, but I am sure John introduced me to it. It offered a short, heady escape from reality, but it didn't last long. Soon we were experimenting with other "light" drugs like LSD and speed. We took LSD in a capsule; its effect was hallucinogenic. Chewing speed or methamphetamines made me feel like I was flying. They sent me square into the center of my painful past where I relived old nightmares and created new ones. I didn't enjoy them much. I wanted to forget my past: dull the pain, not intensify it!

Soon John moved into a house in a decent neighborhood with the kids and me. Part of the freedom of those days was freedom from a marriage commitment. Looking back, I see what a horrid pattern I fixed in the minds of my children; I see the effects in their lives today of my inadequacy to them in their formative years. When I think of that, it hurts me still. It is one thing to be self-destructive; to dislike yourself so much that it doesn't matter what you do. But when it hurts innocent children that didn't even ask to be born...I can only weep and beg their forgiveness.

I will never forget the first time I found the perfect painkiller. It was a winter night, and the kids were already asleep when Janet knocked. Yannis was with her.

"Come in!" I smiled, opening the door.

"I brought you a surprise," the Dutchman half-whispered, moving to the table and opening a brown bag as he set it down. John came in just as Yannis pulled out the paraphernalia and spread it on the table.

"Wow - looks like a fun night!"

"Yeah, well... We've gotta cook it first," Yannis explained. He took out six wax bags about an inch square, each filled with white powder, carefully folded and stapled. He also had a hypodermic needle for the four of us. "Nik, you'll especially like this, I think," he smiled.

"I don't like needles," I replied, doubting his confidence.

"It's worth it, man. When this stuff gets into you, you won't even remember the prick," he assured me, opening one of the tiny bags and pouring powder onto a slip of metal. He heated it with a lighter until it melted into a sticky puddle.

"Here," he said, sucking a bit of the heroin into the needle. "Find a vein, shoot it in, and relax."

I did. I felt numb, not in a trance, but beyond it: into a carefree state where nothing mattered. Unlike the "uppers" I had tried, this was euphoric. It didn't seem important now that my heart and soul had been shattered into crumbles by people I had trusted. I was bigger than they were when I was riding this "horse." No one could find me here, touch me or hurt me.

Heroin became my lifeblood. John followed me into the trap. We were "getting off" (shooting up) many times a day, and the habit started costing more than we could bring home from legitimate jobs.

"Let's go to the shore," he told me one morning after the kids left for school.

"I gotta go to work," I responded, wondering why he'd suggest such a thing on a workday.

"To heck with your 'job,' Nik!" he growled, looking me in the face. "We need more cash if we are gonna continue to enjoy this," he said, pointing to the lamp where our stash was hidden.

"What did you have in mind?" I asked.

"Abandoned cars along the shore. You be the lookout, and I will lift the stuff we need. Pawn shops don't ask questions," he said, smiling.

"You think it will work? What if we get caught?"

"Look, baby," he started, pulling me into his arms, "I know we can make more this way than working our butts off on the assembly line. We'll be back before the kids get home, and you can stay with them while I hock the stuff. I can get twenty or thirty dollars per item, and some are worth more. Easy, baby. Trust me!"

We went to the shore.

"Virtually impossible to get caught! Look at them: they're all asleep!"

Little alcoves like this one dotted the coastline. The parking area was secluded from view by palmetto trees and scrub brush. They were almost private beaches; only three or four cars at a time could fit amid the foliage, through which years of foot traffic had worn rough paths. Unconcerned sunbathers dozed about a hundred yards away. All I had to do was watch for cars or pedestrians who might notice us. The police didn't frequent here, so it wasn't likely we'd be apprehended.

A blue '68 Rambler was his target. He slid a flexible metal band between the window and its weatherstripping, then hooked it across the lock button. John was quite adept at his craft. It occurred to me to wonder if he had been practicing, but desperation prevented my vocalizing this curiosity. Within seconds, he was in the car. He disappeared under the dashboard where he felt and yanked wires, removing the radio, a tape player, and a CB. Then he looked for purses or loose articles in and under the seats. He yanked open the glove compartment to find an expensive pair of sunglasses and a wallet. It was easy to get to the trunk; just push the back of the seat out and have a look. Nothing was in this one; probably the owners had put beach equipment there. John was beside me in less than thirty seconds.

"Let's get out of here," he said as he shoved the loot into my beach bag. He put on the sunglasses and grinned at me. "How do I look?"

"Super," I said. "Probably a lot like the owner! Let's go." We made it home before the bus came, and John took the cache to a buyer. He had to go across town to get more "H" before he came home.

Heroin was an escape at first; a beautiful dream that I didn't want to end. It soon became a necessity. I couldn't get through a day without shooting up several times. What I didn't know in the beginning was the cumulative effect of the drug in one's body. Not only is it extremely addictive, but it also requires increasing the dose regularly in order to achieve the same effect. It wasn't a dream anymore; now it was a nightmare, and there was no way out. My habit was costing me $170 a day, and John's was about the same. It took more than $300 just to keep us in dope, much less groceries, school supplies, clothing and basic life necessities. We couldn't steal enough to live. Our supplier talked us into sharing the wealth. We could make enough and more if we joined him in selling the stuff.

It wasn't a decision I was proud of, even then, but it was necessary. I rationalized that people wouldn't buy from us if they didn't want it. There was no other way to stay alive at this point; quitting was not an option with heroin. People who tried to go "cold turkey" often died as a result. We stocked marijuana, LSD, speed and some other amphetamines, and heroin. Drugs were under mattresses, inside hollow lamps, in cracks between cushions of the furniture, hidden in the walls... When we got a shipment, it was a big one, and the traffic in and out of our home made it obvious what we were doing. Once our regulars knew we had the stuff, it didn't take long for them to deplete the supply. It was true: we were rolling in money, and had all the drugs we needed.

One night after the kids were asleep, I heard a vehicle pull to the curb and stop. Looking through the window, I didn't recognize the car or its occupants. An adrenaline rush sent me to the last place we had hidden some pills. It was between shipments, so the only things we had left were some uppers. I grabbed the bag, ran to the bathroom, and locked the door. No sooner had I flushed the evidence than a voice boomed through the door. I stuffed the empty plastic bag into my bra and went to answer.

"Police! Open up!" I took a deep breath and walked to the door without hurrying. He shouted again...

"Just a minute! I'm coming," I called, slightly agitated. I opened the door and smiled at them.

"What can I do for you, officers?" One of them pushed me gently aside and strode in.

"We've been watching this place for days, and we know you've got drugs in here. We've got a search warrant," he announced, narrowing his eyes. "Now do you want to show us around, or do we need to do some damage?" he asked.

"Look all you like," I said, feigning assurance. "There are no drugs here," I told them.

"Okay, Jimmy. Let's do it." The one he'd called Jimmy turned off the lamp and flipped it over. Nothing. The sergeant went into the kitchen and started throwing open cabinets. He yanked canned goods out of cupboards and let them roll to the floor.

"Hey, my kids are asleep! Could you be a little quieter?" I complained.

"Listen, lady: if I find what you're hiding, you won't have those kids long. Do you understand what I'm telling you?" He glared at me, and I knew he was right. My heart found its way into my throat. I hoped I hadn't forgotten anything!

"Hey, Mike - look at this!"

Oh my God... what...

"What you got?"

"Dang. It's just a candy wrapper." I tried to settle my nerves, and almost prayed the kids would sleep through this. I sat on the couch and pretended to read the newspaper while they went into our bedroom. As they walked through the hall, terror gripped my heart: there were packets of heroin stashed behind the baseboard in one corner of the bedroom. I didn't move; I don't think I even breathed for several minutes. They pulled papers out of the desk and strewed them on the floor. They stripped the sheets off the bed and yanked the mattress off its springs. They turned clothes out of dresser drawers and took everything out of the closet. Even my jewelry box was upended and the bottom removed. Earrings and trinkets littered the floor. I heard Shelley wake up and begin to cry. I went to her room and sang to her until she fell asleep again. I think Chuck was awake, but he didn't get up. To my great relief, after over an hour of searching, they came up empty. I was in the kitchen when they came downstairs.

"We'll be back. You are pushing this stuff, and it is no secret. You got away this time, missy, but don't think you're off the hook. And incidentally - how would you like it if somebody sold this crap to your kids, huh?" There was fire in his eyes. I bluffed the best I could, pretending not to be nervous.

"Just get out. You've destroyed my house, and now you're threatening me? I don't have to listen to this. Get out of my house!"

Without another word, they left. My anger melted into relief as soon as they were out the door. John had seen the car and waited until they left before he came in. I was shaking, both from nerves and from deprivation. He had what I needed. We went to the kitchen and cooked our "fix." Then he flattened the rest of the stack and shoved it behind the wall cabinet in the bathroom. We spent several hours putting the house back together, then had a nap just before it was time to wake the kids to catch the bus.

I have since wondered what the kids thought about all the drugs and about the people who came to buy them from us. The older children never asked questions; when the younger ones did, I told them it was medicine, and they were never to touch it. To my knowledge, they never did.

In spite of my addiction, I was a good mother. I was there for my children when they were home.

We played and enjoyed special outings together. I helped with their homework and made sure they got to school on time. I cooked and cleaned house and made sure they were well dressed. That may sound strange, but it is true. I loved my children, and even when I was "high," I never physically abused them or neglected them. They were my number one priority. The sad part is I didn't know how to love well. I did the best I could with what I had. Hindsight shows me the scars I left on their lives, not by abuse or neglect, but through selfishness. At that time, I was entirely blind to it.

When we moved into the house and found it had a fence, the kids wanted a dog. Since I loved animals too, it was not a difficult decision. Coppertone was a darling puppy. Her coat was a patchwork in shades of brown, and her bright hazel eyes carried a perpetual excitement. Soft, floppy ears perked up at the sound of her name. She and Chuck became fast friends. My son spent hours teaching her to beg, sit and walk a leash. Every morning he fed her before he went to school. One day, though, she got through the gate before he could close it and followed him into the front yard.

"Mommy! Coppertone is out, and I can't catch her. She's trying to follow me. Please come put her in the fence. I'm scared she'll get hurt!"

Chuck had opened the front door and was calling me. I was still in the bedroom in my bathrobe, not at all ready to chase a dog around the neighborhood.

"Go to school, baby. I will come get her as soon as I get dressed."

"But Mommy, she's trying to follow me to the bus stop. Please come now!"

I could hear his voice crack, and I knew he'd begun to cry. I went to the door.

"Chuck, don't worry. I'll take care of it. Now you're gonna miss the bus. Go now. She'll be all right until I get out there. Just 'shoo' her home if she follows you." I wiped the tears from his eyes with the sleeve of my robe and gave him a hug. He reluctantly closed the door. I watched through the window to be sure he went toward the bus. Every few steps he stopped and turned to stomp the sidewalk and shout at the determined dog. She followed him all the way to the corner, and I lost sight of her.

I finished my coffee, dressed and put on my makeup. John had headed out early to Philadelphia for a pick-up. I went to the hall closet, grabbed an old jacket and headed into the yard.

"Coppertone!" I called her name several times, but got no response. I walked to the corner where I'd seen her disappear. No dog in sight. I decided to walk a couple of blocks along the bus route and call her. She'd surely come when she heard a familiar voice.

Rounding the second corner, I saw her laying on her side in a ditch. A sick feeling rose from the pit of my stomach. Her beautiful floppy ears lay in a pool of blood that oozed from the side of her mouth. She was gone. I knelt beside her and stroked her back. Tears ran down my face as I remembered Chuck's loving concern for his pet. I had put myself, my comfort, before my son's need. To passersby, I was just a sentimental woman kneeling in the street, weeping over a dead dog. But from my soul, I grieved something even more precious: the barb of distrust I had planted in my young son's heart.

Life went on in spite of Coppertone's demise. Every two or three days one or both of us would go across the Ben Franklin Bridge from New Jersey into Philly to make a pick-up. We didn't know much about the other people in our "line." We knew our runner, and knew where to go to pick up the stuff, and that was it. We didn't *want* to know any more about the business; it wouldn't be advantageous for anyone if someone in the line was busted.

Sanver City, where we made our connection, was not a savory part of town. Our contacts cleaned, mixed and packaged the drugs in an abandoned set of row houses that had been condemned and scheduled for demolition. The building was three stories high, teetering on a rotted foundation. Paint had once been a part of her facade, but no more. She had been stripped naked by cruel northeastern winters, and her broken windows gaped open like loose teeth in a ragged smile. Yellow signs screamed, "Danger! Keep Out," but the junkies cowering inside had long since become deaf to warnings. The people actually lived in those unsanitary conditions, producing the product I and many others were sliding into our veins: desperation breeding depravation.

It was a Tuesday morning. The kids had gone to school, and we were preparing for a run to Philly.

"I'll call Janet and ask her to stop by and stay with the kids until we get back," I told John.

"You can, but I don't think it'll take that long."

"Just in case. I don't want them here alone."

"Okay, do as you please. But if you're coming with me, put a move on, will you? I'd like to get outta here."

I called and arranged for her to come at 2:30 and stay until we got back. She wasn't busy, so she readily agreed. Janet didn't have children, and she was a wonderful "auntie" for mine.

I grabbed a couple of bags on the way out; I needed a fix in a bad way, and didn't have time before we left. When John stopped for gas, I saw my chance.

"I'm going in," I told him.

"We just left! Is something wrong?" I showed him the needle inside my purse and gave him a look that precluded more questions.

"Okay. I'll pump the gas." I'd become expert at mainlining, and it only took minutes to finish the job. As I came out of the station, though, my heart stopped. Two police cars had ours blocked in, and an officer was cuffing John. I turned to go around the side of the building, hoping they hadn't seen me, but took just two steps when a voice stopped me in my tracks.

"You go ahead," he started, "and you'll never see your children again!" He didn't need a gun. Those words killed my urge to run.

They'd been watching our house, and they knew our car. All they had to do was search me, and they found all the drugs they needed to arrest us on the spot, even without the shipment. I'd never been hand-cuffed before, and it felt strange. I was completely aware of what was happening, but I didn't panic. Maybe it was the heroin coursing its way through my body that made me relax. They impounded the car and took us to jail, and I was deeply ashamed. The only thing that made me feel better was knowing my kids were not alone.

We spent the night in jail. It was the worst night of my life; I was cold and miserable, and in desperate need of the drug upon which my body was so dependent. The local police interrogated us thoroughly, hoping they could get information from us in exchange for an easier sentence. Sometime late the next morning, John's brother sent us a lawyer. He was so irreputable that I don't even remember his name, but he got us a plea bargain with the locals.

"I know you know more than you're telling us," the Chief glared at me.

"I don't *know* the suppliers' names! They don't tell us those things," I insisted.

"Where do you get the stuff, then?" he continued.

"Look, I told you we go to Philly. I don't even know the name of the street." The man looked at John.

"You were driving. You must know the name of the street," the officer demanded.

"Nope. I just go by landmarks," John mumbled.

"What landmarks, then?" the policeman probed.

John swore and growled, "I don't know! Sometimes it's dark when I go. I just remember the turns."

"Don't you get smart, mister," the cop sneered. "This could cost you your next twenty years. Do you get my drift? I'm trying to help you, here. You're not the big fish. I'm after the big one, and if you can lead me to him, I'll let you live to grow up. Do you understand?"

John looked up and nodded.

"Then I guess you'll have to let me take you there," he offered, "'cause you'll never find it otherwise."

"I'll tell you what," the officer started, "you just take us and show us where you get the drugs. If you show us, I'll be sure they go light on you." I hoped he was telling the truth. John stood very still and didn't speak for a full minute. Finally, I think he figured out we were cornered. What else could we do? If we didn't take them to the source, we'd probably go to prison.

"When?" he asked.

"Now. I'll call Philly and tell them to have back-up ready." The officer led us to a waiting unmarked car.

"Climb in, children," he said. "We're going to a raid." His smile was sarcastic, as was his tone. He removed our handcuffs, and we climbed in the back. It was dusk now, and it would be dark when we got to Philadelphia.

Traffic was worse than usual, so it took us more than an hour to get to Sanver City. John gave directions from the back seat, and within fifteen minutes of leaving the bridge, we were parked under a tree just across the street and down two doors from the abandoned row house. Suddenly a shadow clouded the window on the drivers' side. I just knew it was a druggie, and I figured we were all as good as dead.

"Philadelphia PD," he said in a crisp whisper, flashing his badge just below the window. "We have a stakeout going on, and if you don't get out of here you're gonna ruin everything. Leave! Right now!" He was talking to our policeman, who asked a few muted questions and then cranked the car. As he pulled away from the curb, he turned to us.

"You two are the luckiest SOBs I have ever seen," he said. "But let me tell you something. You got off this time, but I am gonna be watching you! And if I see one more car pull up to your door, you're going to prison!" He let us out at the police station and they released our car.

We got home to find Janet alone on the couch. The kids were in bed.

"That was one long pick-up," she complained. "Where have you two been?" I explained the whole horrible scene, and thanked her for taking care of my little ones.

"First thing in the morning, I'm out of here," I told her. "John is going to his Mom's in Woodbury. I am leaving, and I'm taking the kids. I'm gonna make a new start."

"Good for you, Nik. You should do that. This has gotten a bit out of hand," she agreed.

I packed everything into the car that night and got three hours of sleep. While I was packing I considered my plan. I couldn't stay here. The police had threatened us, and I knew they'd never leave us alone. I had no job, no training and little hope for anything that could provide enough income to feed five. Early the next morning, I called Bert. He had gotten back together with Tommy's mother.

"Something's come up, and I need to move. I can't explain right now, but I need to know if you and Barbara can take the boys for a while, just until I get settled. I will take the girls with me."

He agreed without interrogating, and we hung up. I woke the children.

"Kids, Mommy and Linda and Shelley are going away for a while. Em and Chuck are gonna stay with Daddy. I've packed our stuff, and I'll drop you guys off on the way. Now let's eat some breakfast." I poured their cereal and milk in some dishes I'd left out for that purpose and gave each of them orange juice. I found my stash and had a little "breakfast" myself in the other room, then piled them into the car. I left the dishes in the sink. Let the cops wash them!

I put several state lines between the hounds and me and found an apartment in a small southern city. I had enough money to last a while; the drug business had been a lucrative one. However, I really wanted to make a clean start. I tried to get off the "horse." I cut back to once a day, got a job at a mobile home factory, and found a babysitter for the kids just across the street from where I lived. Little by little, I weaned myself off heroin. The craving was there, but I was determined to come clean. But after a couple of months, John came down, and I let him move back in with us. At first, he wasn't using drugs. He got a job at a repair garage for U-Haul in a neighboring town. All was going well. I was thinking it was about time to call Bert and ask the boys to come and join us.

One day I came home from work and went across the street to get the girls to find they weren't there!

"Where did they go?" I queried the sitter.

"Oh, they're fine. Their Dad came to visit them, and he wanted to take them out for ice cream. I figured since he was their dad, it would be all right."

"No!" I shouted. "It *isn't* all right. You should never have done that."

"Why? Wouldn't you have done the same thing? The kids were happy to see their dad..."

"I don't care. I am the one who made the agreement with you to watch my children. He had no right to come and get them. *You* had no right to let them out of your sight! How do you know that was really their dad?"

"Well, they called him 'daddy;' I assumed -"

"You assumed *what*? Anybody could have my children right now! I don't know where they are! *You* don't even know where they are. I am going to call the police, and I am going to tell them what an irresponsible person you are!"

How could she have just let my children go like that? I was totally distraught. Both of us were angry and said things we would probably regret later, but at that moment, all I could see was the faces of my little ones. All I could feel were my empty arms and my broken heart.

As soon as I got home, I called Bert's number. The phone had been disconnected. I called his mother's house. No answer. Then I called the local police.

"I want to report a kidnapping." I talked faster than I intended.

"Okay, ma'am, slowly tell me the details," the voice on the other end requested.

"I left my children with a babysitter this morning - my neighbor - and when I came to get them, they were gone! She said their father, my ex-husband, came and took them!"

"Oh, I am sorry, ma'am. This would be considered a 'family situation.' We don't get involved in those."

"What do you mean, 'we don't get involved'? Isn't it your job to deal with crime? What do you call a kidnapping?"

"Does their father abuse the children?"

"I am not sure," I replied honestly. He had never participated in raising them, so I didn't know what he might do!

"Unless there is a history of abuse, miss, our hands are tied. I am sorry. I hope you find them." The line went dead. She had hung up.

I called the highway patrol and the state FBI, but I got the same story. No one would help me. *So that's the thanks I get for having the girls keep in touch with their dad. That's my reward for the letters I encouraged them to write, for the phone bills I paid so they could talk to him. He just asked them their schedule and where their babysitter lived, and came and got them.*

I contacted people from our distant past, those who had known him as a child in the town where he grew up. People there knew his family, since his father was a minister. Nobody could tell me anything. I didn't know Barbara's friends or her family, so I could get no help there as to where they might have gone. I had full custody of my children. He never gave me an ounce of support for them, so in the years I had them, I was solely responsible for all four. Then all of a sudden out of the "clear blue sky," they disappeared! Much later he told me he did it to protect them, but at that point, there was nothing to protect them from. They had a perfectly good mama taking care of them. I searched and worried, but to no avail. They had disappeared without a trace. Even if he had taken them, how did I know they were still with their father?

When he took the girls, Linda was eight and Shelley was almost five. I was crazed. My precious children were gone. Not through death, but suddenly they were just out of my life. I called Bert's phone and wrote to him, but the line had been disconnected, and the letters were returned. This didn't prove beyond a shadow of a doubt the children were with him. I always worried about where they were, who had them, and what was happening to them. By the time they were taken, John had started using drugs again. I wasn't on drugs at that time, but in my grief at losing my girls, I started drinking. All my efforts to locate them were in vain.

John's drug use escalated, and before long, I had joined him. Life spiraled right back into the pit again, and we found ourselves on the way to our old haunt for a pick-up of a shipment of drugs to bring back. But I had made a decision, maybe the first good one I'd made in a long time.

I dropped John off at his mother's place in Woodbury. "You visit with your mom. I'll get the stuff, then I'll come back and pick you up."

"Okay, Nik. Thanks. I could use a break," he said. I gave him a kiss and took off. *I could use a break, too*, I thought. *A permanent one!*

That was the last time I ever saw John. I picked up the shipment and returned home alone. It didn't take me long to fence the drugs and pay the bills that were pending. Over time, I had been in contact with Mother, and we'd patched things up. She and Tony were living close by, so I moved out of the house John and I had rented and went there. I didn't want him to look for me.

I was sitting in their living room. Both of them were at work and the house was quiet. The weather was gray and drippy outside, and my soul felt the same way. *I don't have my kids. I'll probably never see them again the rest of my life. They're gone. I've no hope for my future whatsoever. Really, no one cares about me, and all I've done is hurt people. Probably the best thing for me to do is just take a hot one and go.* I knew where there was a handgun. It would be easy...

Chapter Seven

Desert Days

*Y*ou don't want to do that yet. I didn't know where the thought came from, but it was enough hesitation for me to pick up the phone instead of going for the gun. I dialed and waited.

"Operator, may I help you?"

"I hope so. I need to talk to somebody, but I don't know who. I am tired of my life, and if I don't get help, I'm gonna kill myself."

"Don't do that, Miss. Please hold one moment, and I will connect you. Will you stay on the line?" Her deep concern was a huge relief. A stranger cared.

"Yes, I'll wait." Not more than five seconds passed before a voice answered.

"Spectrum Programs, this is Jeff. May I help you?"

"I called you instead of killing myself. What is Spectrum Programs?"

"We are a drug rehabilitation facility. Are you an addict?"

"I've done some stuff, but I wouldn't say I'm an addict," I answered defensively. I was a little offended by his frankness.

"Listen, lady, I don't have time to play games. Now you called because you were desperate. Are you gonna be honest with me, or do I hang up this phone and let you finish the job?"

"Okay, yes, I am a junkie." The very words shocked me as I heard them. I'd never thought of myself as an addict before.

"Spectrum Programs is for people who are very determined to get out of the drug scene. It's a tough program, and we don't put up with cheaters or smart-alecks. How serious are you about going straight?"

"I need to make some changes," I admitted.

"Look, ma'am: if you're serious about changing your life, we might consider admitting you. You can't come into our house still dirty. You clean up your act and prove that you are really committed. Then show up on our doorstep in two days and we will talk about getting you into one of our houses." He softened a little as our conversation progressed, telling me that I should not commit suicide, but try their program first. He explained that it was at least a year's commitment, and that I would need to be off drugs in order to register. I couldn't be needing detox, because they didn't allow that in the houses where other residents were living.

"Can you come clean and get here in two days?"

"Well, I'll try." I was high while we were talking, but I had been sporadic in my usage since John and I had been together again, and was not yet to the point where detox would be necessary. My body craved the drugs, but in my heart I didn't want to be that person I had become. Maybe this would be a fresh start. All I knew was that I had to try.

Two days later, I was drug-free, and Mama drove me to the place for my interview. She left me there, but she found out about a parent support group connected with Spectrum Programs and signed up for that. She wanted to do everything possible to help me get my life back on track. Perhaps it was her way of making up for some of the past.

Spectrum Programs was originally founded by a priest. At that time, it was privately sponsored and supported primarily by donations from companies and individuals. We were housed in three different neighborhoods with anywhere from a dozen to twenty-five people in any one residence (depending on the size of the accommodations). There were about seventy people on the combined campuses while I was there. The foundational premise was that drug addicts had lost the basic ability to live a normal life. The program started with fundamental survival skills, giving us tight boundaries around every activity: restrictions that forced us into a routine. I was first ushered into a house with eleven other women, two bunk beds in each of three bedrooms. Our house was in a middle class residential area, and from the outside looked like a normal family home. The furnishings were nice, and we were responsible to keep them that way. We had a resident staff member and an assistant staffer in our house as well. As if we were children, they initially stripped us of all responsibility and started us over with the basics. I was told when and what to eat, when to brush my teeth, how to make my bed and even what kinds of other activities I would be allowed to pursue. All of life was regimented in order to help me "own" and manage my time. Drugs would no longer control me. I was empowered, gradually, to take charge of my own routine, and it felt good.

Each of us had jobs. Housekeeping was the simplest work, and was always assigned first to newcomers. The staff was kind, but strict. If you broke the rules, you would be dismissed from the program. Every day we were required to attend "confrontation groups." In these therapy sessions, members critiqued each other and commented on everything from personal hygiene to bad attitudes. Junkies can tear one another to shreds verbally, and I didn't want to make any enemies in that place.

One session, I arrived early. Some of the others were there already. Dan and Salina were the two I knew best, and they were chatting quietly as I arrived.

"When did you hear about it?" she asked.

"He ran yesterday, and they found him this morning," Dan answered.

"Who? What happened?" I slipped into the circle and interrupted the gossip.

"Some new kid. I don't even know his name," Dan started. "Been here about two months and just decided he'd had enough. Left in the middle of the night. Police called this morning to check; seems he had a Spectrum Programs ID on him. Dead; overdose."

"Man, that's scary. I'm sorry for him."

"It ain't gonna happen to me!" Salina chirped. "I'm stayin' here 'til I got no taste for the stuff. I plan to live my life, not check out of it!"

Others had joined the circle and the staff member, Lorraine, indicated we should start. Hector, another resident, was leader of our fifteen-member group.

"Veronica, seems you been slack on your chores. Some of your housemates ain't happy with you." He stared at her, and she stared back.

"Well, I don't think that's so big a deal, comin' from you. You'd as soon lie as look at anybody. You think I'm slackin'? Well then, you get off your fat butt and come help me!" The rest of the group laughed. Hector just stared at her, unimpressed.

"You clean up your act, Missy, or we can throw you out the door, and you can hit the street," he said, emotionless. "Somebody else will be happy to take your seat." With that, he gave her a wicked smile and turned to his next victim.

"Anybody got any suggestions or complaints?" He hardly hesitated to allow for an interruption. "If not, I have one. Freddie, those breeches you're wearing were made before you climbed to your current size. Would you please requisition some new threads? If not, I am gonna personally come and dress you tomorrow. Who agrees?" Freddie didn't speak, and under his Miami tan, I couldn't tell if he blushed. The group nodded, and some gave wolf whistles and catcalls. It was obvious the vote was unanimous.

After a while, the discussion got deeper than chores and clothes. Ruthann talked about her horrible relationship with her mother. She cried, explaining how she realized she'd been blaming her own poor decisions on her mom. She got sympathy and praise from the group, and Salina rose and gave her a hug. Marty said he'd been thinking about turning in his supplier, and asked for advice. Dan expressed concern that he'd be completing the program soon and was afraid of returning to the "outside" and getting involved with his old friends again.

Finally the session ended, and we all retreated to our own respective houses. I was exhausted, but I knew the meetings were helping me. Hearing about the dead runaway fueled my determination. I wanted my story to be different. After all, I was here because I had decided life was worth the effort.

As the months passed at Spectrum Programs, I learned the system. One climbed a ladder of responsibilities with independence at the top. In the beginning, my only job was personal hygiene. After a few days, I moved into housekeeping, and started taking responsibility for my own room as well as for some common areas. Further up the ladder were tasks in Grounds and Maintenance and Food Preparation. One of the most coveted positions was in the Acquisitions Department. In that office, residents phoned donors, who offered anything from bags of concrete mix to food or linens. We scheduled pick-ups and deliveries, kept records, wrote thank-you notes and took inventory. All of us rotated into various positions, depending on how many were needed for the job and upon our behavior, adjustment, attitudes and progress. We also earned or lost points toward "fun nights" when we would go as a group to a movie, skating, or bowling. Sometimes we received tickets to a wrestling match or the races. Those opportunities motivated us to good behavior and encouraged us to complete our obligations. The Acquisitions Department organized the outings and arranged for free tickets.

When a resident was ready for "phase out," he or she would be allowed to go with a partner to job-hunt and do employment interviews. I never got that far in the program, because after four months at Spectrum Programs, Mr. Robson called me into his office. My stomach was in knots. I couldn't figure what I'd done to be in trouble; I had thought my progress was good.

"Sit down, Nikki," he offered. I couldn't read him; he neither smiled nor scowled. "You've been here four months. How do you feel about the program?" Did he just want my opinion? I wondered if it was too early to breathe relief.

"I think it is just what I needed, sir," I replied. "I am feeling a lot stronger and am hoping life will be different when I get out of here."

"That's what I want to talk to you about. I wanted to tell you about another opportunity you might be interested in. I understand you have a family. Is that right?" The knot tightened. What was he getting at?

"Yes, sir. Four children."

"And you have a police record for selling narcotics. Is that right?"

"Yes, sir." My face was hot; I knew its color rivaled that of my hair.

"Nikki, there is another program related to this one, but more intense. It is called *NARA House* and it is a six-month commitment. If you are interested in this, you will have to be placed there by a judge and agree to go through the entire regimen. It is rigorous, and when you finish the in-house hours, you would still be required for one year to agree to periodic urine tests to be sure you stay clean. This would be while you are living on your own, hopefully holding a job and leading a normal life."

"Why are you telling me about this?"

"I can see how determined you are, and I want you to succeed. I also know that you are divorced and that you don't currently have control of where your children are."

"No, sir," I said as tears spilled down my cheeks. "I don't know where they are. They were kidnapped a while back by their father, and I don't know what happened after that." He waited while I cried and then dried my eyes.

"Nikki, if you go to *NARA House* under judicial order and complete the program successfully, your police record will be sealed, and you will have a clean start. That is the best part of this program. No one can ever hold that record against you again."

I looked at him in amazed disbelief. "Are you telling me that it will be as though I never had that record?"

"Yes ma'am. That's the beauty of this program. It is a kind of reward the government offers for true rehabilitation."

No judge could look at my record and deny me my children. No employer could hold it against me. No one could talk behind their hands about my past.

"Count me in," I said, smiling. "Where do I sign?"

Chapter Eight

Searching for Seed

Freedom is never free. The months at *NARA* House were the most difficult of my life, but freedom from the bondage of drugs was worth every moment of agony I felt there. When I was finally ready to resume life in the real world, I moved in with Mother and Tony. A new chain store, *Doctors' Pet Center*, was hiring, so I got a steady job. Personnel from *NARA* made occasional stops at the store to ask me for urine tests. I always passed, and I was very proud of that. I was truly drug-free at last. I soon worked my way from salesgirl to assistant manager. It was a low-stress job, and I loved helping care for the puppies, kittens and birds. Animals could love you unconditionally no matter what you'd done or been through. I was hungry for that, and I still hadn't found anyone in my life who could offer it.

Not long after I moved in with Mom, I got acquainted with Mike, who lived across the street with his mother. He was tall, attractive, mysteriously quiet and very polite. He was older than me, and his hair was already a brilliant white. I found in him a listening ear and a shoulder to cry on about my missing children. They'd been gone for more than two years. He said he'd help me find them.

One afternoon, I came home from work and found a note on the coffee table.

"I know I haven't talked to you for years and years," Mama's scrawled handwriting said, "but I have something really urgent to tell you. Please call me at this phone number..." It was signed "Dottie." I knew immediately it must be a girl I had known growing up; she was the only "Dottie" I could think of. It was an in-state number, so I plopped into the armchair beside the phone and dialed it.

"Hello?" she answered.

"Dottie? This is Nikki. You'd left me a message, and you said it was urgent. I hope I have the right number."

"Oh yes! Nikki, I've got a story to tell you. I was walking in the mall one day last week. It was just a few days ago, actually. You're never going to believe who I bumped into."

"Well," I said, a bit agitated by her enthusiasm, "I'm not in the mood to guess, so who was it you bumped into?"

"Bert, Barbara and five children!" I was stunned.

"Excuse me? Did I hear you right?"

"Bert, his wife and five kids."

"Where did you see them?" My agitation had vanished; I'd caught her exuberance.

"At the local mall here in my town. We sat down, had coffee together and chatted. We didn't even mention you. I asked him how I could contact them because I had kept your last letter. I thought it was outrageous what he'd done. I was furious. But of course, I played cool and friendly and got all his information for you. Go ahead and get a pen, and I'll give it to you."

"Okay - hang on." I dropped the phone into my chair and stepped to the desk. Rifling through the top drawer, I grabbed a pen and an envelope and ran back to the phone.

"Okay, I'm here. Fire away." She gave me the phone number and the address. My hands trembled as I wrote, but I could still read it. I thanked her as tears ran across my face. I hung up the phone and wept for joy as the evening sun cast shadows across the wall. Tomorrow I would see my children.

The next day, Mike drove me to the neighboring county, and we searched for the address. By the time we found it, it was mid-afternoon. We pulled to the curb as a school bus stopped in front of the house. There were my children! Chuck got off first, then Em, Linda and finally Shelly. Tommy was among them as well, but my eyes were fixed on my offspring. I was relieved to find them and to know that they were well and were living in a stable routine, but my heart ached for them.

I knew I couldn't go to the door that day. Bert would have made a scene. When the kids were inside the house, Mike pulled from the curb, and we headed for home. I would call and talk to Bert.

The next day, I did just that. Butterflies danced in my stomach. It rang six times before a little voice answered.

"Hello?" a young soprano called into the phone.

"Shelley, this is Mama."

"Mama? Mama! Are you coming to see us, Mama?" That was all she got to say.

"Is this Nikki?" It was Bert, and his tone was less than friendly.

"Yes. I finally found where you were hiding the kids, and I want them back," I told him.

"Fat chance of that! You're a dope head and an alcoholic. No addict is gonna raise my kids," he growled into the receiver.

"Look, I have been through over a year of rehab for all that stuff, and I am clean. Even when I was using, I never hurt those kids, and I always provided for them. I love the children, and they know that. Bert, I want the girls back, and the boys, too, if they want to come home."

"If you try to take these kids, I will see you in court," he shouted, slamming the phone into its cradle before I could answer.

I was clean. I had worked hard to get that way and to start over again. No one was going to deprive me of the prize for which I had invested a year and a half of my life! Looking back on it, I can see God's hand in Bert's decision to take the girls. That loss pushed me to the edge and forced me to get the help I needed. If he hadn't done it, their mama's story could have been a lot different. At the time, though, it didn't make reality any easier. The government had destroyed my record, but Bert hadn't. He even brainwashed the kids to tell the court that they didn't want anything to do with their mother. Over and over again we went to court, and it was a similar scene.

"She is a drug addict. She was using illegal drugs right in front of these kids! She is an unfit mother," he would insist. Judge after judge wouldn't even hear my side. "You're right. She has no right to those children whatsoever."

But I wouldn't give up. It took two years before I was even given permission to see them. And then, slowly, I got visitation rights. One day, I just decided I'd had enough. *You know what, I'm not gonna do this anymore. I'm not gonna just visit and leave them without at least offering them the alternative.*

So during my next appointment with fifteen year-old Chuck, I said to him, "You know what, sweetie, I know you're not happy 'cause you've told me you're not. Any time you want to move away from your father, you just come right on." Within a month, he had moved in with me. Not long after that, Bert called.

"You know, I guess maybe you'd better come and get your youngest child because she's incorrigible. We can't control her and she just doesn't fit in, so you just need to come get her."

I can still see nine year-old Shelley standing in the supermarket parking lot where we'd agreed to meet. He dumped her off to me with two paper bags full of clothes and without a word, got in his car, shut the door and left. I bent to brush back her hair from her face and kissed her on the cheek. It was damp. I squatted and faced her.

"Hi baby," I lifted her chin in my hand, but she didn't look up. "You know, Shelley, Mommy's made a lot of mistakes, but I've been working hard to change some things. Let's make a fresh start. I want you to be happy and have a good life. I love you, sweetheart."

She finally looked into my eyes. A moment later, her arms were around my neck, and we were both crying.

Within the month, Linda called and asked if she could come live with us. I had bought a five-acre tract of land in the country and put a mobile home on it as a temporary measure until I could save enough to build a house. Eventually, Mike and his mother moved in with us. Now, my family was complete. The girls shared a room, and Chuck claimed the foldout couch as his bed. Mike's mother's suite was on one end of the unit, and ours was on the other behind the kitchen. It was a comfortable arrangement.

Bert had put Em into a private school, so he didn't live with either of us. From the time he was a toddler, Emory was different. He loved to dress up in his sister's clothes. Sometimes he'd put a towel around his head and say, "See Mommy? I have pretty long hair like Linda!" As he grew and it became obvious he had effeminate tendencies, his father would make derogatory comments: "Gimme that towel, you little faggot!" I will never know what went on during the time the four of them were living at the boarding house, but I have often wondered if there were sexual activities that affected his homosexual persuasion. By the time he graduated and moved to New York and into a career in the entertainment industry, Em had made his choice: he was openly gay.

Just before I bought the property, I had started working in a nearby hospital as a nurses' aid. During that year, I decided to continue my studies and get my license. Having dropped out of school in ninth grade, I had little preparation for continuing education of any kind. However, I took the GED on a challenge and passed. The next fall, I started taking courses to prepare for a two-year nursing program and cut my job to part time. However, after one year, it was possible to earn a license and since I needed the money to support my family, I stopped going to school and started working full time. Mike was great financial assistance; he helped with the trailer and land payments, but I still had the children's needs to consider.

Although Mike's fiscal help was good, the relationship had started to sour. Over time, his drinking became constant. Before he had his morning coffee, he went for the vodka and drank two or three shots. He carried a flask with him on the job and nipped at it all day while he did his survey work. His mother was an alcoholic as well, and would aggravate Mike until the smallest things escalated into a fight.

"Michael, I fixed dinner; why don't you go eat it?" she queried.

"Well, I don't want any right now. I'll eat later." He was transfixed in front of the TV with his bottle. In a few minutes, she nagged him again.

"Michael, you haven't eaten yet! You need to eat!"

Mike shouted some curse from the living room and told her to stay out of his hair.

"Michael! Could you watch your language? Shelley is in the next room doing her homework," I reminded him, irritated at their childish fuss.

"Then tell her to move," he countered. "Can't a man have a little peace after a day's work?"

This kind of dialogue became the rule rather than the exception. Home had become a battlefield, and the children were getting accustomed to shouting as the base level of communication. He and I had been together several years, but out of convenience more than love. I'd had enough. One Saturday morning, I helped the children pack their things and told Mike we were moving to town, closer to the kids' school and to my job. I left him the trailer and the land; he'd made most of the payments anyway.

We moved into an apartment near the school. By that time, Linda was doing well as a high school freshman, and Shelley was in sixth grade. Chuck was begging me to let him quit.

"No, you can't quit school, but you can do one of two things: you can get a GED, or you can go into the military. There are your options."

He didn't like either, but he did get a job. For another year and a half, he still tried to do school. Finally, he joined the Navy. Later while in the military, he got his GED and taught electronics. But I am getting ahead of myself. There is another chapter in that year and a half, and had that one ended differently, my son would probably be a criminal today....

Chapter Nine

Blackened Horizons

By the time we moved into the duplex, Mother and Tony had been divorced for several years, and she had married Bill. He is the only man I will ever consider my "Dad." He loved me, treated me with respect and offered me sound counsel and solid emotional support. From Bill, I learned what a loving father could be like. He would be my knight in shining armor for this chapter of my life.

Our duplex was a haven of rest compared to the air of combat in the trailer with Mike and his mother. It was one of eight units in our small neighborhood, not far from where Mother and Dad were living. They were members of a local club, the Moose Lodge, and sometimes would invite me to go with them to a special function or to dinner. It was during one of these delightful occasions that I met Renzo.

"Good evening, Bill," he said to Dad in thickly accented English. *Italian?* I wondered.

"Good evening, Lorenzo," Dad returned with a smile.

I was sitting across from him at the table. Mother had gone to the restroom. Dad nodded toward me, and offered introduction.

"This is our daughter, Nikki. Nikki, Lorenzo." The gentleman smiled, stepped toward me, took my hand, and kissed it.

"I am delighted to make your acquaintance, lovely lady. And please – call me 'Renzo'," he said. I smiled and fumbled for words. No one had ever kissed my hand before. He was quite charming!

"Thank you, sir. You are too kind," I responded, feeling my face flush.

"Won't you join us, Renzo?" Dad asked. "My wife will be back momentarily, and I am sure she will happy to see you again."

"Not tonight, Bill, but thank you. I am meeting my family for dinner."

"I didn't realize you were married," Dad said.

"Oh no, I am not. I am meeting my brothers and some friends."

"I see. Next time, perhaps."

"Yes, but before that time, would it be all right if I call on your beautiful daughter, Nikki?"

"Why, Renzo, she is an adult. You can ask her yourself!"

"But in my country, friend, you must always consult with the Papa first," Renzo told him.

"Okay... Certainly you have my permission to ask her. She will have to answer for herself."

I sat motionless, wondering what in the world to say to such an exchange.

"Well? Will you consider me a suitor, Miss?" he asked in my direction.

"We can have dinner sometime if you like," I suggested, smiling in spite of myself. He nodded and smiled.

"Thank you. I will call soon. Goodnight." With that, he turned and walked to the door to meet someone. I guess it was his brother.

As he walked away, Mother returned.

"Was that Renzo ... I can't think of his last name...?"

"Yeah, and he asked me for permission to date Nikki!" Dad told her.

Mother laughed and then realized how loudly she had done it. She recovered her composure.

"Why did he ask *you*?" She was still grinning in disbelief.

"That's the way they do it in his country. He's real 'old school' I guess," Dad said, and glanced in the direction of Renzo 's table. "Looks like several of his brothers live here," he noted.

"Isn't he Italian? Catholics always have big families," Mother remarked. The food came, and I was glad we dropped the subject.

The next Tuesday, Renzo called. With his enchanting accent, he asked me to dinner on Friday. When he picked me up, he brought a bottle of wine and a dozen roses. That night, he invited me to a concert on Sunday, and when he arrived for that date, he was carrying a corsage and chocolates. He was wasting no time.Renzo was not handsome. He was shorter than I, and a bit heavier than he needed to be. But although his black hair was never quite in its proper place, his heart was. On Sunday when he brought me home, he met the children. Linda, Shelley and Chuck were all there. They all wanted to hear stories about his life in Sicily, and Linda asked him to teach her some Italian words. I made coffee and watched while he won their hearts. He insisted they call him "Papa."

"I drive a truck across this big country," he said. "Next time I come back home from a trip, I will bring all of you presents. Would you like that?" Chuck wasn't interested in presents, but he wanted to see the truck.

"Okay, I will take you for a ride in it. How about that?" Now he had Chuck's attention, too. I liked this man more and more.

Renzo was as good as his word. The following week, he made a trip to somewhere up the East Coast. During the five days he was gone, he called every night and sent me flowers twice. When he returned, he parked the truck on the street in front of the house. He hopped out with a big bag and came to the door. Shelley opened it before he could even knock. He knelt down, and she threw her arms around his neck.

"How is my little turtle-dove?" he said in between kissing her on the cheek. She took his empty hand and led him into the house.

"Linda! Papa's here, and he brought something for us," she called.

"Now how do you know I brought you something?" he asked her, his eyes twinkling.

"You said you would, Papa. What's in that big bag?" she asked seriously.

"Well, you are right." Inside the bag was a new Barbie doll for Shelley, earrings and a necklace for Linda, an exquisite model of his truck for Chuck and a sweatshirt for each of the children.

"You will make them think it's Christmas," I teased him.

"You all are like my family," he said seriously. "I love you all." The children all thanked him and went to their rooms to finish homework. He pulled out a smaller box for me. Inside was a fabulous emerald broach.

"Oh my... This is too much. Renzo , you can't give this to me. There's no telling how much this cost!"

"It is worth not half as much as I feel for you," he said tenderly and wrapped me in his arms. I returned his passionate kiss.

"Can you stay for dinner?" I asked him as he loosened his hold.

"Yes, but soon after I must go because the truck needs fuel, and I have another trip early tomorrow." When he left, he took Chuck with him in the truck to the gas station. Chuck was enthralled. After that, he spent a lot of time with Renzo in the truck doing local runs, going to ball games; Chuck had found a "dad" in Papa Renzo .

I was smitten, and I realized he was playing for keeps. He loved my children, and he obviously had good intentions toward us. Nothing indicated addictive behavior; I'd lived with that and was all too familiar with its symptoms. Because he was Catholic, sex before marriage was out of the question. He never offered to move in with us – although I gave him a key – but stayed in his efficiency apartment on the other side of town. It was not uncommon for me to wake up in the morning and find him slumped over the armchair in the living room, having arrived in the middle of the night and awaiting breakfast. Over the several months that followed, he installed bolt locks on our outside doors and frequently asked if there was enough money to pay the bills. He sometimes slipped me a fifty "just to help out." This trucking business paid well, and I was happy to be the bene-ficiary of such generosity; it sure helped with our household expenses. The emerald broach wasn't the last magnanimous gift. In fact, the chunk of diamond he put on my finger as an engagement ring was almost too heavy to be comfortable! Needless to say, the kids were delighted.

One morning after I had the ring, Dad called.

"Nikki, could you meet me at the Lodge for a cold one? I need to talk to you."

"Sure, Dad. I'm off tomorrow. What time?"

"Come at 2:00. We'll probably have the place to ourselves."

That seemed a bit odd, but I didn't question him. Dad always knew what he was doing.

I arrived at the scheduled time and found him sitting alone in a far corner of the building.

"What are you doing way back here in the dark, for goodness sake?" I teased.

"Honey, I need to talk to you about Renzo. Sit down."

I obeyed. He wasn't kidding. We ordered our drinks and the waitress walked away. Dad looked at me.

"I want you to know word has it that Renzo is Mafia," he stated, staring into my eyes.

"What?" I could hardly keep a straight face. Finally I broke into laughter. "I'm sorry, Dad, but that is ridiculous," I told him.

"Well, honey, you know me. I wouldn't tell you something unless I felt really confident that my information is correct."

I knew he was right. He didn't gossip. He didn't say anything he didn't mean, and he never said things that in his heart he wasn't sure about. I squirmed in my seat.

"Come on, Dad, you're kidding me," I insisted.

"No, honey," he replied. "It comes from a pretty good source. What I'm saying is this - when you're making any decisions that affect you and your family, think about what I'm telling you."

Our drinks came, and we changed the subject. Dad wasn't mad at me and didn't insist on anything. He just gave me information and left it up to me what I'd do with it. I thought about it a long time. It just didn't make sense. Renzo was kind, generous, devoted, honest... or was he? Being the bold person I am, I decided I'd just ask him.

That night he came in for dinner. The kids had gone to a movie, so I had the house to myself. I set the table with linen and candles and my favorite china. The meal was perfect, and Renzo brought wine to top it off. When we had finished, I said, "I heard a rumor that I need to ask you about."

"Okay, what?" He looked up at me and waited.

"I heard you are involved with the Mafia."

"Who told you that?" he asked, taking another sip from his goblet. He'd skirted my question.

"It doesn't matter who told me. My question to you is, is it true? Are you part of the Mafia?" I wouldn't be sidetracked.

"Nikki, you know how the movies and the media have built up that stuff over the years! Why are you asking me such a silly question? Besides, if I wanted you to know what I do in my business life, I would tell you. All you need to worry about is the fact that I drive a truck."

He had denied it in a roundabout way, not really saying "no," but not affirming either. I wanted to drop it, not to find out any more, but I couldn't. I became more aware of things: how long he was gone, his time spent with the kids.... One night I asked Chuck about their time together.

"Son, what do you and Renzo do when you go off at night?"

"Well, he's showing me how to do stuff."

"What 'stuff'?" I queried. As he explained their conversations and activities to me, I suddenly realized that my son was learning how to con people out of things! Renzo was teaching him how to forge names and other petty larceny activities. I was livid.

"*What* do you think you're doing? Chuck! You know Mama never raised you to do stuff like that. Why didn't you tell me this in the beginning?"

"Well," he said honestly, "You didn't seem to be too upset about me spending time with him, and you seemed to trust him. So when you gave me permission, I figured you knew."

"Charles! I *don't* know this stuff. What do you think? I go to work all night, I sleep all day. What do I know?"

"Well then," he said with teenage candor, "Maybe you need to talk to Papa about it."

At that point, I knew I needed to confront Renzo and find out the truth. The next time he came to the house, the kids were at school. I was pushy.

"I need to know," I said, staring at him, "What are you doing?"

"Listen, the fewer details you know, the better off you are." He raised his voice, and the muscles in his throat tightened into thick cords.

"You need to stay *out* of my *business*!" His face was tense and his fists clenched. I had never seen him this stern, especially with me. I was frightened, but didn't dare show it.

"I am the man of this family, and I am going to marry you. You and these children will be my family. What I do in my business is *my* business. You are not to ask me about it. You are not to be a part of my work, and that is all you need to know. Now I don't want to talk about this any more."

I was not finished. "Well, we're gonna talk about it, 'cause when you bring my child and my family into it, then it affects me. And I don't care what you think! You are *not* taking my child and teaching him

137

to be a criminal!" I was shouting, and tears were puddling in my eyes.

"I am not teaching him to be a criminal; I'm teaching him the business."

"No, you're teaching my child how to be a criminal. That's the way it is. You may see it differently, but this is the way I see it, and my child is not gonna be a part of that. I want you out of my house *now*!"

"Oh you do, do you? Well, you know, that's not exactly the way it's gonna happen." He leaned toward me and squinted his eyes.

"Yes," I argued, calm and collected now, "That's the way it's gonna happen!" I slipped his ring from my finger, and threw it in his direction, hitting him in the forehead with it.

He didn't say a word, but turned and picked it up from the floor. He walked to me, took my hand, opened it and put the ring in my palm. Closing my hand around his promise, he said quietly, "I'm going now. I have an appointment. When I come back in the morning, I expect all this conversation will be behind us, the ring will be back on your finger, and that will be the end of it." And with that, he walked out the front door.

Some women might have been scared into submission after that warning, but not this redhead. He had a rattlesnake by the tail, and didn't know it. Nobody talks to me in that attitude and gets away with it.

A few days went by, and Dad called me again. "We need to talk. I'll meet you at the Lodge at 2:00 – and you be there. We have to talk today!"

I found him in the same spot. "What's up?" I asked him cheerfully.

"You know my friend, Ted?" Dad asked as I sat down.

"Yeah..."

"You know he's a lawyer?"

"Yeah, I know he's a lawyer. Doesn't he have an office over near the courthouse?"

"Yeah. He has a certain client he told me about."

"And?" I was wondering where this was leading.

"Nikki, you don't understand. This client is a mobster. They call him 'the Boss.' He heads up a family in this area, and the person you're engaged to is part of that family. He is a mobster."

"All right, but I already broke it off with him." So what was the big deal?

"No, honey. You don't understand. This same man who was engaged to you last week has put a contract out on your life this week."

I was dumbfounded.

"Well just how would you know a thing like that?" I asked him, wide-eyed.

"Because Ted is always a part of their meetings. He takes notes, writes up minutes and makes certain that every task that's brought up in the meeting is performed by the person to whom it is assigned. When Renzo came into their last meeting, he walked in, put money on the table along with *your* picture and said, 'I want her hit.' Ted told me Renzo most often does that kind of work himself, but in this case, for him to take the assignment would be out of order.

Secondly, he might have a hard time doing it because of his attachment to your family."

He paused to let his words sink in. My head was spinning. He loved me one day and could really kill me the next? Dad continued.

"Renzo said he wanted a contract on you. When Ted picked up the picture to add it to the minutes and looked at it, he passed it over to the Boss and said, 'I know this woman. She's the daughter of some dear friends of mine, and whatever is going on here is a personal issue.' So the Boss said, 'Well, we don't do this kind of thing,' and he tore the picture in half and handed it back to the attorney. He handed Renzo his money back and told him, 'We don't do this kind of thing. This is not what we do. We don't murder mothers of children.' Then Ted said the Boss added, 'We don't beat 'em up and hurt 'em, either.'"

Dad was silent. Neither of us spoke for an eternal minute. Finally he said, "Honey, I just thought you needed to know. I don't know what you should do about it, but if we can help, you don't hesitate to call, okay?"

I assured him I would. I didn't feel like talking any more, so I hugged him goodbye and went home.

Only a day or two later, in walked Renzo as though nothing had happened.

"What are you doing here?" I demanded. "I don't want you here. I meant what I said! You need to get your sorry carcass out of my house!"

His voice was steady. "I told you it's not over."

"Well," I replied without hesitation, "Maybe it isn't in your little guinea brain, but in my heart, it's completely over, and you need to get your little body out of my house and away from my children. And *don't* come back. If you do, I'll hurt you."

He just looked at me, laughed and walked out the door.

A few days after I had thrown the ring at Renzo, my car had died. It was old, and was becoming a money pit, so I decided to look for better transportation. I wouldn't ask Renzo for help, so I scoured the paper for a car. I had some money, enough for something used, and I was determined to stand on my own. I called the number and met a man named Fred, the owner.

The second time I went to see the car, it was almost noon, and Fred asked me to lunch. I liked the car, so over lunch we made arrangements for me to make monthly payments and buy it. Then he asked me to dinner. During the next week and a half, we had several lunches and a couple of dinners together. I told him about breaking off with Renzo and what my Dad had said.

"Hmm," he said, and laid down his fork. "Seems to me a little protection around you right now couldn't hurt anything."

I smiled at his kind intentions. "I don't know that I need it, but I'm open to whatever," I replied. I figured I could take adequate care of myself. I had gotten pretty good with both a rifle and a handgun while we lived in the country. I used to shoot occasional rabbits and squirrels and cook them for dinner. I could keep up with my son in target practice, and felt very comfortable knowing that if something happened, I had both a handgun and a pump-action rifle at my disposal.

In fact, I had pulled the rifle on Renzo already. It happened one night before he had tried to put the contract on me. In fact, this just might have pushed him to pursue it. That particular night, I didn't have to work my 11-7 shift, so I was in bed early, right after I tucked in the kids. It must have been about 9:00. I was awakened from a sound sleep when Renzo opened my door and flipped on the light. He'd never been in my bedroom before, and I was startled. From my half-sleep, I could see his frowning face and hear him accusing me of being ungrateful and owing him a hearing. I don't wake up well, and this was not what I needed in the middle of my night off.

"Will you get out of here and leave me alone? I really don't want to talk to you under any circumstances, much less now. Just go away." I managed to say that coherently.

"You wake up and answer me. There is no excuse for your behavior after all I've done for you! And what about your kids? I would be a good father to them, provide for them. Wake up and listen to me!" He shouted the last line just as Chuck appeared in the doorway behind him.

"What are you doing?" my son's agitated voice asked. "My mother told you to get out of our house and leave us alone!" I was fully awake now, leaning up on one elbow with the bedclothes across my body. Here was my son becoming my hero. What happened next gave me temporary insanity. I see it all in my mind as though in slow motion. Renzo reached with his left arm, made a half turn and pushed Chuck back a few steps.

"Get away, kid. This is not about you."

It wasn't a violent shove; he didn't shout nor did he hurt my son, but maternal instinct coupled with my redheaded Irish temper took over. I flung the covers back while reaching with one motion for the gun in the corner. What made this lunacy was the fact that I didn't wear pajamas; they were too confining. Leaping to my feet, I pumped the rifle. Poised, stark naked, in the center of the bed with my copper hair awry, I pointed my twenty-two right at Renzo's chest. He was strangely speechless.

"Mother!" Chuck called in wide-eyed shock.

"What? You—go to bed! You—get out of my house!" I screamed back.

"Mother—your clothes!"

I didn't move. "All right with the clothes," I said, still aiming the gun at Renzo.

"Okay, I'm going. I'm leaving," said the intruder, and he did. I can imagine his frame of mind upon laying my picture in front of the Boss.

So when Fred suggested I could use a little protection, I went home, loaded the pistol, and tucked it carefully in the crack between the arm of the chair and its seat cushion. I left it there only when I was in the house. Since the kids knew it was my chair and never sat there, I felt safe enough.

One night after I learned about the contract and had shared it with Fred, I was sitting in that chair watching TV, waiting to go to work. The children were asleep in their rooms when a car pulled up. I flipped on the porch light. It was Renzo. I returned to my seat and slid my hand into the crack to feel the pistol. Since he knew I was still up, he knocked instead of using his key. He was a criminal, but a polite one.

"Who is it?" I asked, as if I didn't know.

"May I come in?" he asked.

"Yes," I said, pulling the pistol to easier, yet still invisible, reach. I had told him I would hurt him, and I'd meant it. He unlocked the door and didn't make four steps before a deafening ROAR almost burst our eardrums! Three spotlights flooded my living room. In a flash, a gargantuan man dressed in black almost ripped the door off its hinges, and he and two others just like him landed in my living room and hovered like grizzly bears over poor squatty Renzo! Each wore a gun on his hip, a scarf on his head and black leather from the neck down. But for missing eye patches, they could have been pirates right out of an Errol Flynn movie scene. One of the giants spoke.

"So tell us, Nikki, are you having a problem here, or what?" He was speaking to me, glaring at Renzo, and I'd never seen any of them in my life! Renzo backed up.

"Well, as far as I know, there's no problem here," Renzo managed. He eased in reverse right out the door. The men watched until he left, then dissolved into bellows of laughter. I joined them, and we all laughed until tears streamed down our faces. Finally, one of the three spoke.

"We're members of 'the Saints,' a local motorcycle gang. Fred called and said you might need a little help out here, so we've been staking out your house, 24-7, all this week. We got that loser's address, his car and truck tag numbers, and we've just been hanging out, waiting for him to show. Harleys can be pretty loud, and we were depending on that to slow him down. Looks like it worked."

"I'll say," I was still in awe, feeling like the proverbial damsel in distress after a rescue by a superhero.

"If you need anything, just let us know," the spokesman told me. He didn't give me his name, but he wrote a phone number on a slip of paper. "Call anytime. We can be here in minutes."

I was glad it was time for me to work; I couldn't have slept after that adventure! The next morning was Sunday. I had not been home long and was cooking breakfast for the kids before going to bed when there was a knock on the door. I looked through the window. It was Renzo. This time, he waited, not using his key. I opened the door.

"What do you want?" I asked him.

"I came to return this." He opened his hand and gave me the key. "I got the message. I'm sorry. I meant for you to have a good life. I didn't mean for this to happen. I love you, and I would always have been a good father and good husband, but obviously I'm not for you. I am gonna go away and leave you alone. I promise you I will never bother you again, and neither will anybody I know."

And, true to his word, he was gone. I never saw him again.

Chapter Ten

Pesticide

Strange the tools God uses to accomplish His ideas. Who would have thought that buying a car could be the ticket to my escape from the Mob? If I had written the script, I probably would not have included Fred. Hindsight is always sharper than foresight, though, and in His infinite wisdom, God knew just who to bring into my life and when...and why.

Fred was not handsome, but he was winsome. He had an irresistible charismatic personality. Having spent twenty-nine years in the military, he retired as a colonel, so money was not an issue for him. When we met, he told me he was separated from his wife, pending divorce. He owned a campground and was living there in a lovely cottage.

Fred and I were married in December, 1977, when his divorce was final. The kids and I joined him in the cottage on the campground. We had been married several months before I found out I had actually caused the divorce between Fred and his wife.

I was angry, embarrassed and felt deep remorse; I would never intentionally have been a part of that! But now I was married, and as far as I was concerned, it was a lifetime commitment.

Fred never bonded with Chuck. My son was now eighteen, and Fred thought he should be working and become independent. He encouraged Chuck to join the Navy, and so the boy enlisted. I was delighted at the transformation in my teenager when he came home for his first leave. Formerly he had been difficult to rouse from sleep in the early afternoon, but this new soldier was up by seven with his bed made to perfection and his clothes tucked into his duffel bag. His military commitment launched him into the "real world" and gave him a good start. I was very happy for him.

Linda married young, and was also out of the "nest" before I was really ready for her to be grown up. Shelley married at 15, just as I had. Looking back, I can see that she was reliving her mother's life; Fred's criticism and coldness made her seek an escape route from emotional abuse. My oldest son had moved to New York upon his graduation from high school and was pursuing a career in drama. Fred and I found ourselves "empty nesters." It was strange for me; where had their childhood gone?

We had been married about six months when Fred's son and daughter-in-law came to live on the campground with their young family. I was thrilled to have grandchildren to spoil living so close, and soon took full advantage of it! The older girl was a toddler, and the other an infant, and I was delighted to have children in my life again. Jay wanted a job in a local police or sheriff's department. He came from California to work with his dad in order to take the training, make the application, and settle his family closer to relatives.

I will never forget the first time I saw him. Our living area was L-shaped, and when he walked in the door, I was in the adjoining room. He called out to me, "Hi! My name's Jay. I'm here; I'm dad's 'child.'" He went on with some silliness, but I didn't hear much of it. From the moment he walked in, I was totally smitten! I loved him immediately, but with deliberate desperation squelched my intense feelings. He was a married man with two young children, and I was his father's wife, for goodness sake!

"Well, come on in, Jay," I said. "Make yourself comfortable. I'm fixing some food. Won't you join us? I'm sure you're starving." My heart was beating so fast I could scarcely breathe, and I felt guilty to the soles of my feet for my attraction to him.

For the next couple of months, he, his wife and their kids lived on the premises. Every day, I walked under a cloud of guilt. Each time I saw him, or knew he had entered our house, my heart leaped. He smoked a pipe with some delicious-smelling tobacco that permeated the house. When he'd come for coffee with his dad in the mornings, I would smell that pipe and be out of bed like a shot. Sometimes during the day, I would look out the windows, watching him work. There were twenty years between me and Fred, but only six between me and Jay. *What are you doing?* I asked myself. *You weak, wicked, evil, witchy woman! Stop looking at him. He is a married man. He has children!* I felt like I was going crazy. I was never as relieved as I was the day they left. He had not found a job in law enforcement, so they moved back to California. I had been more successful in *my* quest, though; Jay never knew of my ridiculous, very one-sided attraction to him. I would *never* knowingly be a part of interfering in anyone's marriage. That had been done to me, and I was sickened by the thought of it. He was out of my life, and I didn't have to deal with his presence any more.

Our life in the campground was fun for me. My part of the business was to set up parties, covered dish dinners, game nights and other events for the campers. That was the enjoyable side of life during those years. It wasn't long, though, before our marriage began to sour. I started to see the real Fred, and it wasn't the same face he showed in public. My husband had spent time in Viet Nam, in Korea and in the Cuban missile crisis. He was very familiar with the rotten side of life. Relationships with women had become his outlet for stress. Being married to me didn't cure that habit, but I had to learn it the hard way.

Fred was never physically abusive with me, but his tongue was a lethal weapon. Unprovoked, as though he were just making general conversation, he could push a verbal dagger into my heart, twist it and then sit down and drink a cup of coffee as if nothing had happened. One evening I was sick and went to bed early. The next morning, I found Fred at the table when I came from the bedroom to go to work.

"Good morning, dear," I greeted him with a smile and gave him a peck on the cheek.

"Yeah," he grunted back, not looking up from his newspaper.

"I'm sorry I was asleep last night when you came to bed. I really meant for us to talk for a while. I wanted to hear about your day," I offered.

"No big deal. You're not worth anything in the bed anyway. Just about like a limp dishrag," he noted, taking a sip of coffee and still staring at the paper. "You have absolutely nothing to offer to a relationship; you're cold, callous and calculating."

"What did I do?" I asked, fighting back angry tears.

"Nothing. That's the problem. You can't walk and chew gum at the same time." He chose some four-letter words to describe how worthless I was, and added, "What are you good for, anyway?"

I stared at him, hurt and confused. He hadn't even told me what he was mad about. There was no recourse for this kind of accusation; I had no platform from which to defend myself. I left for work, dumbfounded and hurt.

Several times a month, Fred would find something to accuse me of, blame me for or just verbally hurt me for no reason. I should have seen it as a symptom of a sick, depraved heart. Working out of my own bruised and battered background with whatever internal resources I could muster, I was resigned to make the best of it.

After two years, we sold the campground and moved to the city. I took a job as a nurse at an assisted living facility where my mother was working in the housekeeping department. I worked during the day, but Fred was retired. One day when I got home, he came from the bedroom.

"Well, here's the working woman," he noted, smiling. I was glad to see him in a good mood.

"Yeah, it was quite a day. I'm pretty tired. What did you find to do today?" I asked him, offering a hug.

"I cleaned out the file cabinet and got rid of most of the stuff related to the campground. Didn't take long. Then I just kind of laid around. You know, I think I'd like to go back to work. There isn't enough to keep me busy around here. At the camp, I could always go fishing or something."

"What would you like to do?"

"Handyman stuff, I guess. I'm pretty good at that, and you don't have to think real hard. I'd like working with my hands, keeping busy. Why do you ask?"

"Let me talk to Mr. Hardiman at Bentwood. I think they may be needing somebody in maintenance."

"Yeah? That would be good. We could drive one car to work and have the same hours."

"I'll talk to him in the morning." I felt sure I could get him on there since I had a good work record. Fred could fix just about anything.

Sure enough, the next afternoon, Hardiman called Fred in for an interview, and he started the following Monday. It was a great boost to his ego to be needed by so many different people, and he seemed to enjoy the work. He was available on call to everyone in the building as well as to the various staff. With his outgoing personality, it didn't take him long to know most all the workers by name. After several months, Fred was promoted to Maintenance and Housekeeping Supervisor, making him Mother's boss.

One afternoon, I was at my desk filling out the paperwork for the next shift when Mom poked her head in the door.

"Hi Baby," she said. She wore a strange expression.

"Hi, Mom," I replied, staring at her. "Is something wrong?"

"Nikki, we need to talk," she said flatly. I didn't like the ominous sound of that.

"Okay, wanna come in?" I asked her.

"Not here, sweetheart. Let's go for a walk in the garden and talk there. It will be more private." I closed my books and grabbed my jacket, and we headed for the back door of the building. Once we were down the path out of earshot, Mom stopped and turned to me.

"Nikki, do you know Frieda, that huge blonde who works in dietary?"

"I think so. You mean the one that wears skin-tight sweaters over rolls of body?"

"Yeah, we're talking about the same gal. Well, your husband is having an affair with her."

"*What*? You are out of your mind? Fred? with *her*? Mother, she weighs 350 pounds! You can't be serious!"

"Nik, I have thought about talking to you for weeks. I realize coming to you makes me the enemy because you are trying to keep your marriage together. I know you've been struggling, and I admire that determination. But it's time you knew. Everyone else here knows it, and they've all been tiptoeing around and not mentioning it because they don't want to hurt your feelings. Well, you may see me as the enemy, or you may not. You may hate me for the rest of your life; that's your choice. But I had to tell you. Somebody had to tell you! I am sick and tired of seeing him make a fool of you." She was quiet, watching my face.

"Whatever..." I mumbled, and turned away so she wouldn't see the tears gathering in my eyes. I had played the fool again, and now this worthless man I'd chosen to love was offering his affections to another. I think it would have been easier had she been petite and pretty. It was so insulting to know he'd chosen Frieda over me.

I didn't want to believe it, but I had a feeling Mother was right. There were signs: hairs on my pillow that were too light for mine, an odd perfume on Fred's clothes, lipstick on his collar... my heart closed my eyes and turned off my brain. I didn't want to go through another break-up! Even though I wasn't thrilled about finding the truth, I knew I had to do it. I had to confront him, so I came up with a little plot. I was quite proud of my creativity. The nursing office phone had extensions for all of the other departments in the facility, so I knew I could listen in to anything being said on any line. It was a Sunday, and I was working in the nurses' station while Frieda was working in dietary. Fred was at home when I called him.

"Hello," he answered, the TV blaring in the background.

"Turn it down," I told him without bothering to say hello. He did.

"Nikki, is that you?" he asked.

"Of course, who did you expect, Frieda? Listen, I want you to understand something, Fred. I know all about you and her. I know about you two and your little affair, and flaunting it all around Bentwood trying to make a fool of me. But I've got news for you. The jig is up, dude, and when I come home, we're gonna have it out!" I hung up before he could say a word and just stood by the phone to watch. In less than fifteen seconds, her line lit up. I waited until the button stopped flashing and picked up.

"...oh, my gosh, she knows about us. We're gonna have to —"

"You bet your sweet butt I do," I broke in, "and it's *mine*!"

I slammed the phone into the receiver and took off down the hall for the dietary department. Not five minutes later when I arrived, she was already gone. She didn't let the ground cool nor her tail-feathers drag getting out of that place! I was right behind her. I told the nurse on the other wing I had a personal business emergency, and didn't think I'd be back that afternoon. I gave her my report and asked her to tie up some details, and then I drove home. Things started falling into place as I went. All those weekends he told me he was going fishing with "the guys" in our huge motorhome – that I was working to pay for – taking the boat and trailer, he was actually with her in it.The nights he was working late on someone's plumbing problem, or putting in a new light fixture, he was more likely spending the evenings in the arms of his blonde broad.

Needless to say, by the time I got home, I was boiling over. The motorhome was gone, as was the truck. I assumed he had hitched the truck to the back of the motorhome and run to meet her. *I wonder where they could be*...I only had to think for a moment before it was clear. They'd gone to Mitzie's. She used to be my friend. We played cards with her and her husband. At the same time, she knew Frieda. She mentioned her once or twice when we were together. It made perfect sense to me now; she'd helped them see each other on the side. I would look there first.

Before I left the house, I picked up the phone and called Mother.

"Ma? I just want you to know I confronted them. It's out in the open, and I'm sorry if I didn't believe you. I probably did in my heart. I just wanted you to know what I did, and he's gone. I think Mitzie has been helping them get together. He's probably there. Now I'm gonna go find that SOB, and when I do, I'm gonna blow his brains out. I've had enough." I was teary by now, and Mother was terrified.

"Honey, now don't be doing anything stupid like that," she warned me.

"You know what, Ma? At this point, the way my life is going, I don't really care. Somebody's gonna pay, and I'm tired of paying."

She was saying something else, but I just hung up on her and went out the door.

I headed to Mitzie's house. I always kept a handgun in my bag, and Mother knew that. Unknown to me, she and Dad pursued me. It was a caravan in the blind: Fred didn't know I was after him, and I didn't know Dad was following me.

As I pulled the car into her long driveway, I spotted the motorhome with the truck in tow behind the house. I parked in front. Since it was summertime, the windows were all open, and I could hear scuffling as I got out of the car.

"Oh my gosh – here she comes!" It was Mitzie's voice. They were all scrambling, trying to get out the back way. So I climbed back into the car, drove to the front of the alley where I'd come in, and pulled my vehicle across the opening. Since he couldn't back the motorhome out, he would have to come in my direction in order to leave. *I've got you now, sucker!*

The motorhome started up the alley, and I got out of the car, standing in the open driver's door and looking over the roof.

"Hello," I called to the oncoming camper. He stopped and got out.

"Don't you start anything," he warned, frowning.

"I didn't start anything," I reminded him, "but I'm gonna finish it!"

Just at that moment, Dad pulled in behind me, slammed the car into "park" and jumped out, leaving it running. Mother opened her door and stood up.

"Nikki! You stupid woman – don't do anything rash." He was much closer to panic than I was. "He's not worth it," Dad insisted, tugging at my sleeve and begging me to listen to him.

I hadn't taken the gun from my purse, but Dad knew I had it with me.

"Honey, he isn't worth it," he repeated. "Let it go."

"You're right," I told him, "but I want to have my fun." I took the gun out of my purse and stood there holding it, aimed right at Fred.

"You know," I said to my target, "I want to do this really badly because you're the scum of the earth! But Dad's right; you're not worth it." I put the safety back on the weapon and tucked it into my handbag. "You two can have each other. But you know what? Every penny you have in the world will be mine before it's over, so think about that!" Before he could say a word, I got in the car, motioned to Dad to move his, and went home. I had plans to make.

Chapter Eleven

Running from Locusts

Fred's family owned about half of Bangor, Maine. His father had started a gas company and also owned laundromats, apartment buildings and other properties. I didn't know when I married him the kind of wealth he, his sister and one brother were entitled to inherit. By the time our marriage fell apart, though, I was well aware of what his widowed mother was sitting on, and I knew I could claim Fred's chunk of it. I wanted to find out just what that involved, which would mean going to Maine.

When I had warned Fred I'd take everything he had, he knew I meant it. So when he slunk through the door later that evening, full of apologies and remorse, I wasn't surprised. He was playing into my hand. I had already made up my mind: this marriage was over. I had to do a good acting job, though, if I wanted the reward that was coming to me.

"Nikki, I am really sorry. I acted like an idiot," he mumbled with his head down. Then he looked up at me. "Maybe what we should do is just sell this place and buy another one - maybe go further south, live there and start over... if you're willing..." His voice trailed off. I saw my chance.

"You know what? Maybe you're right," I lied, "Maybe we should. What the hay; people can make mistakes. Before we do that, though, maybe we should just get away for a while. Why don't we go to Maine and spend some time with your family and maybe even go out to California and visit the grandkids... you know, just see the gang. Then we can come back and shop around for some property." I knew there were some business meetings going on in Maine, and I wanted to get more information about what was in the "kitty" for me. I was looking out for number one.

We took off two days later for Bangor. While we were there, we did some hunting and fishing together, and I did some of my own. I found out what I needed to know and got the names of people to contact when the time came without giving away my plan. In early November, before the weather turned cold, we headed for California.

Jay was more gorgeous than ever; he was now walking around in a police uniform. We were there until spring, living in the house with the couple and our darling grandchildren. Fred and I had our own room, but in the process of life, I learned more than I wanted to know about Jay's family. Their marriage had long been in trouble. His wife was a serious alcoholic and refused to admit it. One day I got the courage to talk to Jay about it.

"You know, Jay, your wife is sick. Have you considered getting her some help? Maybe rehab or something?"

"Yeah, I'd love to do that," he answered, "but what can I do? She won't admit she has a problem and won't agree to anything. I'm just about at the end of my rope," he admitted.

It was sometime in March when Jay called her aside.

"You know," he said, "I can't fix this. And if you're not willing to make some changes, I don't want to be married any more. I just don't want to be with you if you're not going to get help."

"Well, what do you want to do?" she asked him without emotion.

"I want a divorce," he told her, hoping to shock her into reality. Instead, she shocked him.

"Fine," she answered. "No problem. I won't contest it."

I was surprised how fast that can happen in California. They made agreements about the house and property and papers were drawn up. We had been planning to leave, but decided to stay to help with the children while they worked things out.

In spite of her alcoholism, we had a lovely visit. She was not a violent drunk, and although she was seldom without a drink in her hand, at times she was reasonable and fun to be around. One night in December – before any talk of divorce – Jay got out his guitar. He played country songs we all knew and some he'd written. I was very impressed with his talent. After that first evening of music, it became a regular event. After dinner and on weekends, we played and sang. Their home was situated on the edge of the desert, and the shrubs on the property bore witness that the wind there only had one direction. Our refuge in the evenings was a cement landing next to the garage on the least windy side of the house. Beach chairs stacked along the wall made it a favorite gathering place, and some or all of us were there most of the time. One particular evening stands out in my mind. It was late April, and his divorce was already in process. Neither he nor Fred had any inkling of my intentions to end my marriage.

"What an incredible night!" I noted as I pulled out a chair and sat down. Jay had been alone, plunking away on his guitar.

"Yeah. On clear nights like this, you can see from one horizon to the other," he said, still strumming. He seemed distracted, so I decided not to ask him to play anything in particular. We were quiet for a few minutes. I knew this would be the last time I would see him, and I hoped he would meet someone wonderful, his own age, remarry and have a happy life. Although I was internally envious, I loved him enough to want what was best for Jay. Finally, I broke the silence.

"How are you gonna deal with all this stuff? I've seen you with those girls; they absolutely adore you. They're all over you from the time you walk in the door at night. This can't be easy for you." I watched his face as he stared into the clear, starry night.

"You know, I can't take the kids away from her. First of all, I don't even know what I'm gonna do 'cause I plan to resign from the sheriff's department. I don't think I'm gonna stay here. Dad's been talking to me about maybe going back with him and getting involved in some kind of business."

They had together turned Jay's van into a deluxe camper, and Fred thought that kind of renovation could become a lucrative business. The camper was luxurious, and I could see the potential of such an idea. I felt a fluttering in my stomach when I thought of him being close by, but I didn't want to interfere in his life.

So I just said, "That's great," and hoped my voice didn't offer more than was intended. He turned his head and met my gaze.

"Nikki, I want to tell you something, and if I'm speaking out of turn, you can let me know. I need to share this with you." I shifted a little in my seat.

"Go on," I told him, not sure what was coming.

"I still remember the very first moment I saw you." The fluttering escalated to pounding.

"You do?" The words sounded like someone else's.

"Yeah, I do. And I'm gonna tell you... when I walked into that house and looked directly across at you - right into your face - and said to myself, *Oh my word! My dad - you lucky dude!* You were - and are - the most gorgeous woman I ever saw in my life. You just made my heart flip over."

Until that moment, I thought my attraction was only mine. Now I was hearing him say it was mutual! I knew it was all right to tell him.

"Well, the first thing I want to say is, do you remember me telling you that your dad and I were not getting along very well?"

"Yeah."

"I'm gonna tell you this, and I hope you will keep it to yourself. I am trusting you with this information. When I get back home, I'm leaving him." Jay smiled.

"You really are?"

"Yeah, I really 'are.'"

"Well, that's a start!"

"And you know what else? You remember that day you walked in my house? I know what you're talking about, because all I saw was you. I have watched you. When you were outside, I'd be peeking through the windows looking at you. I was absolutely smitten! I am still totally crazy about you! And I want you to know I am not expecting anything back from you. I'm just telling you exactly how I feel."

He was still smiling, his eyes fixed on me. I'm sure I blushed.

"Now, that's better than a start, isn't it?" He leaned over and kissed me on the cheek. From that point on, I knew I'd found my soul mate. At that time, though, I still had a husband. Jay was divorced, but I was not. Therefore, we kept our relationship entirely platonic. It was good protection for us and gave time for our friendship to grow.

Not long after that, we packed up and started our caravan. Jay was driving his van, now transformed into a camper, and we were in our motorhome. Every night in various campgrounds, we got side-by-side sites. We usually sat outdoors at the picnic tables singing and talking until bedtime. We were camping somewhere in Texas when Fred and I got into a terrible argument. Jay was sitting in a lawn chair at the table between the campsites with his guitar. Fred was lounging in the afternoon sun. I was inside the motorhome cutting up a chicken.

"Bring me a beer, Nikki," Fred demanded. I didn't understand him, so I went to the door with a piece of raw chicken in my hand.

"Did you say something?" I asked him.

"Yeah, I did. Are you deaf? I said, 'bring me a beer!'"

"Well, I'm trying to get this chicken in the frying pan, and my hands are a bit sticky. Could you come in and get it?" I didn't intend to be sassy, but I guess he thought I was, because it made him angry.

"You little..." he said the rest under his breath, swearing and hurling insults. I heard him, and came down the two steps onto the ground, still carrying the floured chicken thigh.

"Look, Fred, you're already drunk. Why don't you eat something before you drink any more?" I asked him seriously. At that point, he got to his feet and stumbled in my direction. He grabbed my arm and shoved me backward. I didn't fall, but the chicken thigh wasn't so lucky. It lay on the step of the trailer, crusted in dirt. Now I was mad.

"Okay, mister. You can eat that piece!" I snarled, reaching to pick up the nasty poultry. He lunged toward me, fist raised, and I faced him, half standing and half leaning on the step. Suddenly Jay's chair went flying backward and he jumped between his father and me.

"Dad, don't you ever, ever put one hand on her again. I'll kill you if you do," he said evenly. "Treating her like that is over." He was staring at Fred, poised for a fight. Fred stopped and glared at Jay. He used to beat up his sons until one day when Jay beat him instead. Maybe he was remembering.

"So, what's in it for you?" he sneered.

"I happen to be in love with her, and she loves me, and I'm not gonna let her be treated that way any more." Fred turned around and looked at me.

"Oh, I see! You're after my son! Well, I'll tell you what: since I've been such a 'bad boy,' why don't you two just go off and do your little thing? And when you're all done and worn out, then you can come home and be a decent wife!"

"You know what?" Jay interrupted, "I remember when I was a kid the way you treated me, how rotten you always were to me. You are the lowest of the low. You are a piece of work! Nothing but trash. And as soon as we get settled, you are out of our life, once and for all! Don't ever, *ever* come near either of us again." I turned, picked up the slimy chicken and went into the motorhome to finish cooking. At that point, I wasn't sure any of us had an appetite.

Later that night, I was lying in the bedroom, awake. Fred was on the picnic table, not yet asleep, when Jay came to the door of the motorhome.

"Nikki?" I slipped on my robe and went into the living room.

"What is it?" I asked him.

"I want you to come over to my camper."

"No, I'm okay over here; he's not gonna bother me," I told him.

"Well, I am not sure about that. Right now he's drunk and angry, and I don't know what he'll do, so I need you to come over into my trailer." he said, his brow furrowed. I knew he wouldn't sleep at all if I didn't comply.

"Okay," I answered, and went back to the bedroom for some extra clothes. As I followed him to the camper, Fred turned and looked at us.

"Hey, you gonna go off together?" He snorted a laugh. Jay stopped and turned toward him.

"You need to just shut up. You don't even have a clue what loving a person is all about." We went into the camper. Jay grabbed a blanket.

"You sleep on the bed. I'll be right here on the floor." He rolled up in the blanket beside the bed.

"Give me your hand," he whispered, and I reached over the side of the mattress. He took my hand and held it all night while we slept. The next morning when I woke, Fred and the motorhome were already gone.

Chapter Twelve

Locusts Fly

I called Mom and Dad to let them know what had happened. We took our time getting back, stopping to visit Shelley on the way through Texas. She was glad to know I was divorcing Fred, and our visit gave her an opportunity to get better acquainted with Jay.

When we got back, we went to Mom and Dad's place. I still had to get my belongings from the trailer where Fred and I had lived. We'd been home about two days when Fred showed up at the door. Mama let him in, trying to be cordial until the details were settled. Fred sat on the couch and I was across from him in a lounge chair. He stared at me with a strange expression. It almost looked like remorse.

"I've had a couple of weeks to think about it," he started, "and I know that I killed our relationship." He paused, and then continued, "...But I'm sorry. You're my biggest regret, because I've lost a good woman. I just didn't know how to treat her."

I think he was waiting for me to respond, but I didn't, so he went on.

"If you threw me aside for somebody, though, I'm glad it's my son because he's a good man. It's a little bit different situation, but he is a wonderful man even though I didn't treat him right while he was a kid. I don't think you can do better. I hope you guys will be happy." Then he got up, put on his coat, and left.

I went to the trailer one day while Fred was gone and finished packing. Since Jay and I had been practicing some of his musical compositions, we decided to go to New York and try to get some songs published. While we were in the big city, I found a letter in the mail stating that Fred was attempting to push the divorce through in Maine, but he couldn't do it legally because he hadn't been a resident there. He had filed in order to deny me access to his assets. I had postponed legal action until I had an opportunity to put together the alimony package with the benefits I wanted. As it turned out, our peace of mind became more important than the money.

"Honey, in order to get this over with, why don't you just consider letting it all go?"

"Jay, sweetie, do you know what you're saying? There are millions in the pot here! Are you sure you want to just forget your entire inheritance? That money goes back to your grandfather's estate. Is it really a good idea just to ignore it?"

"I think so. Then we won't have to deal with Dad ever again. Otherwise, this could be in and out of court for years, having to face him and deal with all his crap. Isn't tranquility worth whatever it costs?"

In the end, I had to agree with him. I didn't want Fred around messing up our lives, so I just let it go and gave Fred the divorce. It was about thirteen years after that before Jay spoke to his dad again. One day, his aunt called and said his father had been diagnosed with lung cancer. About six months before he died, Jay called him and they talked. He gave him our phone number. After that, Fred and I talked once or twice. He voiced regrets about how he'd treated me.

"It's okay," I told him, "because regardless of what happened between us, I have a wonderful life with Jay. I have the happiness I've been looking for my whole life. And you were the one who made that possible, so that's how I look at it."

Fred remarried a couple of years before he died, and he left everything to his new wife, but that was all right; after all, I had the best of the family treasures.

New York turned out to be a fruitless trip. We had trouble pinning people down to give us a hearing and an answer. Two different agents told us they liked our work, but said we would do better in Nashville. Unfortunately, we had no money for another move, so we went back home instead.

"Let's just play music for a while and see what happens," Jay suggested. He wrote more songs, and we practiced night and day. We were by now happily cohabiting like a married couple. I didn't renew my nursing license, but became a waitress instead. Not long into the job, the bosses at the sleazy little club where I was working found out that Jay and I were willing to perform. The owner offered us twenty bucks per night plus tips. The place was a little country bar, and after a good performance, we could walk out with forty or fifty dollars. Jay worked odd jobs as he had opportunity, and with my waitressing, we were doing all right.

One night during our gig, two strangers walked in. I could tell they didn't belong in the community; they were dressed in suits and ties, and one of them carried a briefcase. I nudged Jay and asked him if he knew them. He shrugged his shoulders and shook his head. We had just gotten some soft drinks and found a quiet table near the wall when one of them approached us.

"We've been listening to you guys," he said, "and you're wonderful! We have not heard better harmony anywhere. This is absolutely great, but you need a full band behind you." We must have looked pretty dumb, because we just sat there and stared at him. I wondered, *Who are you? And what do you know about it?* Before I could ask, he must have read my mind. He whipped out a card and handed it to Jay, who glanced at it and passed it to me.

"B and J Enterprises at your service," he said with a nod. We were still a bit confused, but Jay had the presence of mind to speak.

"So what should this mean to us?" he asked the man.

"We have connections - *good* connections - and what we need from you is a commitment to go to Nashville."

I am sure both our faces lit up, and our eyebrows rose in tandem.

"I want you to meet with someone. I've called him and told him I was coming to listen to you guys tonight."

To this day, I have no idea how they heard of us, but they did. Word travels from little country bars to big wigs in Nashville, so I guessed some kind fan had passed positive comments into the right ears. The scout spoke again.

"I've already called this man and told him about you. His name's Johnny Dollar. He has a recording studio in Nashville. I told him I'd talk to you and call him back if I approved you. Then you will need to go meet him."

We discussed the possibility with him and got more details, then agreed to his proposal. When the conversation ended, the ball was in his court.

"I'll call you in a few days and tell you the next move. Do you have a record or a tape I can hear?"

"Well," Jay apologized, "just some junk we mess around with at home."

"That'll do for now."

I ran to the car, fished out the tape and gave it to our new advocate. When he left, I realized I didn't even know his name! He could have said it, but after he mentioned Nashville, I didn't hear anything else. True to his word, though, our anonymous angel called a few days later.

"Johnny is looking to see you guys as soon as possible. He's very excited about it."

It didn't take us long to prepare for the interview. We jumped into our van, which had been serving as sleeping quarters most of the time anyway, and headed to Nashville the following day.

Johnny Dollar was a bulky middle-aged man with a car-salesman smile and shiny shoes. He took us through the studio, pointing out gold albums of some of his former clients hanging on one wall. *Yes! This is a dream come true!* Jay gave him some of his previously copyrighted music, and we also brought him another tape. He took us into his office, put the cassette in and told us to sit down. After the first song, he stopped the tape and faced us.

"Oh, my gosh! You guys are on your way," he declared with assurance. My heart beat wildly in my chest, and I noticed Jay's smile.

"What I need to do... Hmm, I need more fullness here. I want a better sound than this. So what I need to do is get you back in the studio with the musicians behind you so we can get a couple of demos done. You're not gonna be ready for a long time, though, so don't think that you're going to pop in the studio and in three months, you'll be making a million dollars. That's not the way it happens. First of all, I've gotta polish you up, get you the way I want you, get the look I want... all this happens first. We need 8x10 glossies so we can start getting you out there; enter you into contests...."

He was chattering away about music writing competitions, about judges seeing and hearing our music. "It's a long process. It can take a year or two or longer. But you need to live here. I need you here in Nashville."

"Okay, fine - we're here!" Jay answered for us both. "We just have to go back home and get our stuff."

"That's fine; no problem. But you're gonna need a job, because until we can put this all together, you're not gonna get any money. We have to work with this. I'm willing to put the money into backing you, and I'll do all the things it takes to produce your music, the image... all those things. But your personal finances are your own responsibility."

He was straight with us from the beginning. I knew we could trust him, so that very day we went out and got a job at a campground. It was a smart move; we worked on the campground, and they provided our living space and a small salary: sixty-five dollars a week for the two of us. I worked in the office collecting the money, and he did maintenance. We arranged to begin work in two weeks. That would give us time to go back, gather our belongings and return to settle in.

It was a hectic two weeks, closing our affairs, packing up what little we owned and heading to Nashville. We left Mother and Dad on Easter Sunday and spent that night on the road in the van. The next morning when we arrived, we were so excited we could hardly keep our feet on the ground.

"Let's stop before we go to the campground and call Johnny," I suggested, "just to let him know we're here and find out when he wants to meet with us."

Jay thought it was a good idea. We found a phone booth at the next exit and pulled out his calling card.

"Hello. Could I please speak to Mr. Dollar?" Whoever answered didn't recognize Jay's voice. "This is Jay. Mr. Dollar is expecting my call..."

I could tell the person on the other end of the line had interrupted. Jay's face clouded and he turned away from me. Something was wrong. I stepped away from the door of the booth, wondering what it could be. Finally Jay hung up the phone. He stood inside the enclosure, shaking his head. Finally he faced me, but he wasn't happy.

"What is it? What's wrong?" I asked him, trying to pick up a hint from his face.

"That was Johnny's brother. He said Johnny shot himself yesterday. He found out over the weekend he had incurable cancer, and he just went to his apartment and killed himself. That guy was cleaning out his office. He's closing the business."

Johnny didn't consider how many lives he would take with him when he put that bullet through his

176

head. Jay and I stared at each other. Tears streamed down my face. Grief for our new friend was mixed with grief for a lost dream. Anger about the present and fear of the future lurked in the self-pity that gripped my heart. Jay took me in his arms, and we stood in front of the phone booth clinging to each other. Finally he spoke into my hair.

"I guess we should go on to the campground and start the job. We'll just take one day at a time and see where they lead."

"Okay," I whispered, still holding him tight. "I'll follow you."

Chapter Thirteen

Barren Ground

Our campground job included living quarters: a lovely trailer in the woods in a little town called Goodletsville. We had a motorcycle to use for daily transportation into the city, so our expenses were minimal. If Johnny Dollar had been impressed with us, surely someone else would be! On our days off we would explore. We sang wherever anyone would give us a hearing. Unfortunately, in Country Music City, we were not the only struggling artists. Competition for attention was fierce.

One weekend, we heard about a song-writing contest. Jay had composed a ballad called *The Wrangler*. The words painted a glorious picture of the cowboy's life. Everyone who saw or heard the song loved it, so Jay decided to enter it.

We were sitting in the registration office, palms sweating, with several other songwriters. Finally someone opened an inner door.

"Are you Jay?" a kind lady asked.

"Yes ma'am," my sweetheart replied with a smile.

"Come with me, please." I followed without asking permission into a giant office. Plush beige carpet and dark paneled hallway opened into a spacious room. A man in a suit rose from behind a wide desk.

"Jay," he said, rising to greet us and taking Jay's hand, "I am Adam Forsyth. I'm very glad to meet you." He shook my hand, too, but continued to talk to Jay.

"Your song, *The Wrangler,* is the best I have seen in any category: love songs, country rock, ballads... It was the best piece that's been submitted. There's only one problem. For radio use, it is far too long. You need to go back to the drawing board and shorten it. If you do, you'll make millions - even if you don't sing it! We can give it to an artist who's already known, but you will make lots of money on this. Would you work on it and get back to me?"

"Sure! I can do that. Thanks so much for your encouragement, Mr. Forsyth. I'll be back soon with the revision," Jay assured him. We went home ecstatic. Hope was rekindled. We could make it big in the music business...

For days we pored over the song. We tried cutting verses, lines, words... Nothing worked. Since it was a ballad, it told a continuous story. To our great disappointment, we struggled to no avail. The song simply could not be shortened and still maintain its meaning or emotion. In the end, the award went to a writer whose composition was more commercially acceptable. Jay was crushed; someone else had walked away with "his" prize.

The next day, I was in the sales office talking with my colleague, Claudine.

"Yeah, it was heartbreaking, all right. To get that far and then miss the 'brass ring' by just a couple of verses. That's a great song. When Jay wrote it, he thought about how ideal it would be for a voice like Willie Nelson's."

"Nikki!" She turned toward me so suddenly I was startled.

"I've got a friend who has been a close buddy of Willie Nelson's since they were children. They used to get under car hoods together when they were teen-agers, before either of them was famous. You should talk to him. His name is Fred Carter. He's June Carter Cash's brother, and he is a studio musician. Plays with Willie sometimes." She was talking fast in her excitement.

"I'm sure that would be a good contact, but he's not gonna talk to us. Anyhow, we can't just walk up to the door and say, 'Hi. Wanna hear our song?'"

"Why not?" she insisted. "He's just an ordinary guy. He only lives a few blocks from here. He's been on a lot of recordings and plays and travels with Willie. Go and let Fred hear it, because if anybody can get it into Willie's hands, his best friend can!"

Her optimism and enthusiasm won me over, and I talked Jay into finding his house. As Claudine had said, Fred was accessible. Unlike Nashville's elite, Mr. Carter lived in a house with no gate. We walked right up to the front door and rang the bell. The owner himself answered.

"Hello," he smiled. "May I help you?"

"We hope so," Jay started. He introduced himself and me and explained what had happened about *The Wrangler.*

"Listen," he said, "My office and studio is around the house at the back. Why don't you kids walk around there and come into the studio, and I'll listen to your song."

"Great. We'd be glad to do that," Jay answered as we stepped into the yard, and our host closed the door. Once we were out of sight around the corner of the house, Jay grabbed me at the waist and swung me into a two-step.

"We're on our way," he whooped as he spun me in a circle and I landed in his arms. "Nik, Willie Nelson's best friend is gonna hear our song! We're in! This is so incredible!"

I pushed back from his chest and tousled his wavy hair.

"Oh, my gosh, Jay! You've done it! We're here, and this is it!"

After a few minutes of laughing and crying, we regained our composure and proceeded to the back yard.

Between the house and Mr. Carter's studio was a porch complete with rocking chairs and potted plants. I opted to wait there while Jay went in to play the cassette for Fred. I could hear the music through the wall, but couldn't make out their conversation.

After a few minutes, Jay came out to have a cigarette. Mr. Carter followed him, talking.

"I am sure when Willie hears this he will be in contact with you. What a great song! I'm going to send him the cassette and then try to call and get in touch with him. If I hear from him, I'll let you know."

He went on to tell us if we'd like to send him the song also, be sure to flag it so that Willie would know it was from him. He told us how to package it and to send it to Willie's Pedernales Studio in Spicewood, Texas.

As soon as we were out of earshot, I could wait no longer.

"What did he think?" I asked Jay.

"He loved the song. He sat with his back to me in the studio, hunkered over the sound system, but I could tell he enjoyed it. When it was over, he said, 'I'm gonna call Willie right now.' But then he hesitated. 'You know, I think he's doing a tour for Farm Aid at the moment. I'll call his mother.' Nik, he called Willie's mother 'Mama.' I heard him find out Willie was in the Pedernales studio, and then he tried to call there. Whoever answered said he'd already left on the tour. He said, 'You wouldn't believe the crap that comes across my desk. When I hear something like this... wow. When Willie hears this, he'll record it.'"

We left him knowing that we were going to hear that song on Nelson's next album. To our great disappointment, we never heard from Willie Nelson or anything else regarding that contact. I am convinced that the artist never heard the song. Maybe the tapes didn't arrive, or someone tossed them in the garbage bin without giving them to him. It had been another build up to a dead end.

Shortly after that, another offer dropped into our laps. Not far from the campground was a rustic country restaurant. Although it was old and quaint, it was very popular. They served food and also had a bar. On evenings and weekends, various artists played there. Most of them were exceptional musicians. This restaurant decided to produce a radio show on site, and they asked Jay and me to be regulars on the program. Again our hope peaked. Finally, perhaps we had a foot in the door! A week passed, and we stopped in to ask about the plans.

"Well, we're not quite ready for broadcasting," the owner told us. "Come back in two weeks." So we waited. Two weeks later, he told us there had been delays, and it would be at least another month. We waited, and waited, and waited. We were getting tired of being disappointed. For months we'd been in this city and still had nothing to show for it. With no savings, we were living hand to mouth. Finally, Jay had had enough.

"We're going to leave Nashville," he announced one evening after we had finished dinner.

"I don't think that's a good idea," I countered. "If we leave, then we're never coming back."

"Yes, we will. We just need to go somewhere, get a good job, save some money - a few grand - and then pursue our music."

"No, Jay. You don't understand. All my life I've tried to get into music. Since I was a child singing on the radio, it has been my dream. That 'brass ring' has always been just beyond my reach. This is the last straw. I am not gonna leave and then come back. We are either going to stay and see it through regardless of how hard it gets, or we are leaving. We are either gonna burn for this thing, or not. Without 'the burn' it won't happen. And frankly, my embers are dying."

He stared at me. In addition to the musical doors being slammed on us at every juncture, his boss had been giving him a hard time, and Jay thought he was getting ready to fire him. If we lost our jobs with nothing in reserve, we would be homeless as well as hopeless.

"We're gonna leave," he said with finality.

"Fine," I answered with resolution. I think he planned to soften me and persuade me to rethink, but as life carried us on, the tide never returned us to Nashville. We decided to go back home. Later that night, though, Jay phoned a friend who lived in Dahlonega, Georgia.

"Hi, Michael. This is Jay."

"Hey, man! How in the world are you doing? I haven't seen you in ages. Where are you living now?" his childhood buddy answered.

"We're getting ready to leave Nashville and head south," Jay told him.

"What were you doing in Nashville?" Jay explained the long story, and then paused and turned to me.

"Michael wants to know if we'd like to come through Dahlonega and see how we like that area. I could work with him in the stone business, he says. What do you think?"

"It's okay by me," I told him.

The following day, we turned in our resignations and packed the van. That night, we started south. A day later, we were with Michael and his wife, Carolyn. They offered us their partially finished basement as our living quarters, and Michael suggested Jay consider a partnership in his stonework business. Since Carolyn also worked full-time, I agreed to stay home and to do the cleaning, cooking and laundry.

Jay and Michael were working almost daily just north of Atlanta, and though the traffic was minimal at that time, the commute was still more than an hour each way. We had little time together. We ate all our meals with our hosts, and even spent time with them on weekends. More than a year later, tension was building between the two men, and the partnership was proving to be quite unbalanced. Jay decided we should move into Atlanta and find a place of our own.

One day he came in and told me, "Honey, they're building these brand new apartments about twenty miles from here in Alpharetta, and we got lucky! I asked the lady to hold one so we could go look at it this weekend. Would you like to see it?" At that point, I was ready for a change.

The apartment was perfect, and although we had nothing to furnish it with, we decided to accept it. We took the little TV from the camper and bought a small table, two stools for the snack bar in the kitchen and two beach chairs. Our bedroom consisted of a mattress on the floor, a clock, and a lamp. As I think back on it now, the months we lived that way were the happiest of my life to that point. I told Jay we'd remember starting out together there and miss those days. I was right.

One night during those first months there, the phone rang after we'd gone to bed. It was Emory. His calls were infrequent, so I once teased him about being my "wayward son." He enjoyed the joke.

"Hello," I answered, my voice a little sleepy.

"Hi, Mama. This is your wayward son," he said.

"Em! I'm so glad to hear from you. What have you been up to?"

"Same ole, same ole, Mama. Just doing some music now and then and acting in a couple of small productions. It's enough to keep grub on the table."

He always hesitated to brag, but I knew how exceptionally talented he was. I could picture his angelic face wearing that wonderful, perpetual smile.

"How are you guys doing?" he wanted to know.

I told him about the apartment and about Jay's construction work. We'd talked during a previous call about Nashville. As an artist, he was one of the few who understood our deep disappointment with the music business.

"Mama, I've got some news to tell you about." The pitch of his voice lowered a bit, and something in me knew it wasn't going to be pleasant.

"Okay, honey," I said, "what is it?"

"Mama, I'm HIV positive."

For a moment I couldn't speak, but I knew I had to say something.

"You know what, son, there's a lot they don't know. Are you sure?"

"Yes, Mother. I've been tested twice. But I'm only HIV positive. It will never have to go to AIDS."

"Well then, that's what we're gonna hope for, Em. You eat right and get enough rest and take care of yourself, and you'll be all right."

I changed the subject, asking him about the drama he'd done recently. He seemed relieved not to continue the conversation about his troublesome news. After that, he kept in closer contact; we talked at least once a month, and he went on with his life and career.

Jay went to work as an independent contractor. Building and fixing things were second nature to him, and he enjoyed it. Our apartment was situated in town, so I didn't feel isolated when he was away. One day he came home with an invitation.

"This guy at work, Roger, asked if we'd like to come to a little party at his house Friday night. What do you think?"

"Where does he live?" I wasn't in the mood to drive to downtown Atlanta to party with a bunch of strangers.

"Just over here in one of the townhouses. I think he said there was a business opportunity involved."

"Yeah? Well, I guess it couldn't hurt."

That Friday night we showed up at Roger's and found ourselves at an Amway promotional. We probably met thirty people that night, but in my mind, only one stood out. Actually, two people were in the spotlight: John and his wife, Lydia. John was a likeable person and easy enough to get to know. But his wife, Lydia, was a piece of work! From the moment we met, we had a mutual unspoken agreement: the further the distance between us, the better we were going to like it. Lydia had an attitude I couldn't pinpoint, but I had the feeling she wished I would disappear. If she was in the crowd when I approached, she would leave. I couldn't find one thing to like about her, and I didn't try very hard. Oil and water are a more agreeable mix than the two of us were. Jay and I signed on that night to become Amway distributors. To my great horror, I learned that Lydia would be my supervisor.

"Jay, I can't believe we are going to have to interact with that woman!" I complained to him on the way home. "She is such a goody-two-shoes!"

"Maybe you'll like her once you get to know her," was his response.

"Humph! I doubt it. She just seems so... she's unbelievable! You know, most people I can tolerate or just walk away from, but with her, I just want to say, 'Come over here. Let me smack the snot out of you!' I'd be very happy if I never saw her again!"

Every single week, I had to talk to Lydia to order my Amway supplies.

"Hello, this is Lydia!" she would chirp in her happy soprano.

"Hi Lydia, this is Nikki," I would return.

"Oh." Nothing else.

"I just have some stuff to order," I'd tell her.

"Okay. What do you need?" I'd read her my order and she'd write it down.

"All right, thank you." Then there was a dial tone. It seemed she hated me as much as I despised her. One day when Jay came home, I grumbled to him about her again.

"You know what, Jay? I know we want to build this Amway thing. I think we are gonna have a lot of fun with it, but *that woman.* She is such a stickler for all this paperwork. Everything has to be done according to the 'rules.' I have to 'call this person, sign that form, fill out that order just so...' I never met anyone so insistent on the letter of the law. She's intolerable. Honey, I can't promise you I'm not gonna tear her face off, Okay? Every time I talk to her, I get a little angrier..."

"Just grin and bear it, Baby. John's a sweetie; we both like John. Just give her a wide berth."

That's exactly what I did. If we had to be together at a meeting, we stayed on opposite sides of the room, and if one moved, the other countered to keep our distance. For almost two years we lived in a private cold war.

During that second year, we started shopping for a house we could buy. We knew it was time to stop paying rent, but our savings were meager – certainly not enough for a down payment. One day, Jay came home with wonderful news.

"Nikki, somebody told me today about a friend of his who has a house; his fiancée has a house. He wants to unload his and move into hers since it's bigger and she has kids. His house is in Woodstock. I told him we'd come by this weekend and have a look."

We bought the place on a lease-purchase and moved. A short time afterward, I dropped Amway. At last, the cold war was over. I wouldn't have to see Lydia ever again. I expected she was just as relieved as I was about that.

As it turned out, we bought the house at a good time; we soon needed more space and more privacy than the apartment would have allowed us. Death was coming to visit.

Chapter Fourteen

Mourning in the Desert

We'd been settled in the house for about a year. I was working as a nurse in a rehab facility and Jay was in the contracting and remodeling business. One night he came home totally distracted. "What's wrong honey? What's bothering you?" I asked him.

"I am just so tired of 'up and down the line' with that plumb bob. There has got to be a better way to get things straight than by using that awkward piece of stone-age technology. That thing slows me down and causes me to lose my temper just about daily."

"Well, what are you going to do? Are you gonna sit here and complain about it, or just be quiet and let it go?" He looked at me with a strange expression.

"That's a good question. I don't think I like either of those options. I'm gonna make something better," he answered.

I wasn't sure what a "plumb bob" did, but I knew that if a better one could be invented, Jay could do it. He had both a logical and a creative bent, and was just stubborn enough to keep working at it until he had a solution. About a week later, after scribbling and doodling in all of his spare minutes, he brought me a piece of paper.

"Here it is," he announced, and showed me his invention.

"That's great, honey! What is it? What does it do?" I queried.

"I call it a 'thing-a-ma-bob.' It will take the place of the traditional plumb bob in allowing a carpenter or engineer to get a line straight. This thing should sell like hotcakes."

"Well, then I think we should get a patent on it," I told him.

We tried. Every place we inquired, somebody had his hand out for money. When we found out how much a patent would cost, we just rolled up the idea, got a notary to seal and sign it, and put it in a file drawer. The patent would have to wait.

In the meantime, life went on, and we let the thing-a-ma-bob simmer on the back burner. We were finally planning our wedding. We'd been together almost seven years; it was time to make it official! But as we were making plans, we decided to postpone them. My attention was needed elsewhere.

During those two years since Em had first told me he was HIV positive, we'd talked frequently. He always insisted he was fine and life was beautiful. He had moved to California and was enjoying the nicer weather. Suddenly, though, his situation changed.

An ongoing sinus infection took Em to a new doctor. Whether by intent or through neglect, he didn't tell the physician about his diagnosis. The medicine he prescribed sent my son into full-blown AIDS. The nightmare of repeated infections and hospitalizations became routine. Finally, they put in a shunt to give him his medications because his veins were too collapsed to take an injection. For a while, a feeding tube also became necessary because he had difficulty swallowing. At that point, he called me.

"Mom," he said, "I want you to come out for a visit. We need to talk."

I agreed, went to California and spent ten days with him. He told me what he needed me to do, how he wanted it to end, what he expected for me and what he had written in his will.

"Em, do you want to go back with me? I will help you pack..."

"No, Mom. Not yet. I still have things to do; there are too many loose ends to tie up, so I need to stay here a little longer. When I can't do it any more, I'll call you."

I left him there in June, 1990. In October, he called.

"Mother, I can't see. Only shadows. I am trying to muddle around in this apartment, and it's not good. I need to come stay with you."

"That's fine, son. Your room is ready. Do you need me to come out there and help you move?"

"No, I have a lot of friends to help. I'm gonna stay in close touch with you. I just know I can't do this alone any more, not if I can't see."

I hardly recognized the skeleton of the man my son had become. His skin was wan and his green eyes glazed, but his smile was just as it had been since he was a baby. One day he called me aside.

"Are you here, Mom?"

"Yes, Em, in the chair across from you. Did you want to talk?"

"Yeah, I need to tell you something. You know, if I had my life to live over, I'd do things differently. I realize now that there was a better path than the one I chose. Mama, I've become a Christian, accepted Christ as my Savior. Jesus has something to offer, and I'd like to know you will be in heaven with me, too."

"I'm glad for you, son. It's important that you have your peace. I'll think about what you said," I told him.

I did think about it, but not in the way Em had hoped. I thought at the time his decision was a desperate attempt on his part to obliterate some bad choices and their consequences. I was glad for him, but I'd already seen religion. It hadn't worked for me in the past. If God was out there, he was certainly not acting on behalf of my son!

As the months passed, the disease affected his brain. Alzheimer's complicated the AIDS, and I learned to speak to him simply, as I had when he was a young child. At night when he cried out for me in pain or fear, I'd jump out of bed, slip into my robe and curl up with him in his bed, holding and comforting him until he went back to sleep. At Christmas, we had a family reunion, and all of the kids came home.

We knew it would be the last holiday we'd ever have all together. Em surprised us by singing a song he'd written while he was in New York. He didn't forget one word. For a moment, we could pretend he wasn't gradually leaving us.

One night early in the new year, I heard Em's voice.

"Mama... Mama..."

I went to him and stayed until he fell asleep. No sooner had I crawled back in my own bed again until I heard, "Maaa..." His voice trailed off.

I went through the dark hall into his room and took his hand. I gently shook it; he wasn't moving. I turned and flipped on the light, then hurried back to his bedside. Pulling him from under the cover, I realized he wasn't breathing! Hysteria overtook me, and I screamed at him.

"Breathe, damn you!"

Jay and Chuck appeared in the doorway.

"Call 9-1-1. They have to wake this baby up." I was weeping hysterically, holding Em, rocking him in my arms. I didn't remember any of the things he'd asked me to do. I couldn't let him die. I wasn't ready to lose my child. Hot tears coursed down my cheeks and soaked his t-shirt.

The paramedics came almost immediately. They thought he was dead. I thought he was dead, but one of them asked, "Lady, what do you want us to do?"

"You bring him back!" I shouted hysterically. "Bring him back or I'll kill you! You bring him back to me..."

They did, and I have regretted that ever since. They moved him to the hospital, barely alive and comatose, where he lay for ten days. He had asked me to let him go, and I could not.

I lived at the hospital. I didn't leave his side. On the tenth day, the nurse called me to the phone. It was Jay.

"Nik, I'm coming over to the hospital to get you. You're coming home."

"I can't, honey," I told him.

"Nikki, you have to come home. You need to put your feet up for a while and rest. You have a family here that needs you, too."

I knew he was right.

"Please don't make me leave," I begged, tasting tears in my throat.

"Just for a little while, baby. Come home and rest. Sleep in your own bed until morning." I reluctantly agreed. Going back to Em's side, I leaned over his bed.

"Honey," I talked to him as I had been the entire week, "Mommy's gonna go home and just be with the family a little bit. I'll take a shower and sleep, and I will be back in the morning."

Suddenly he raised his head off the pillow and his eyes popped open!

"Mama," he said in a very loud bass voice, "are you gonna be all right?"

"Yeah, baby. I'm gonna be fine. It's okay." I was shocked by his sudden response, but pleased that he had spoken to me. I settled him back under his blanket and tried to reassure him.

"I want you to know something. Your Mama will love you through eternity, but I realize you're suffering. I know you're hurting and sick, and if you want to go home, Mama will understand." Now I could let him go. Tears welled up and spilled down my cheeks as he went to sleep. Jay arrived, so I slipped out and left Em resting.

I had just settled into the recliner in the living room with a cocktail when the phone rang.

"We need to go back to the hospital," Jay told me.

I knew Em was gone. We had his body cremated, and I brought the urn home and put it in the closet. Jay thought it ironic for me to do that.

"Em would laugh if he knew you kept him in there," he teased. "I can just hear him now: 'Mom, I spent years trying to come out of the closet, and then I die, and you put me back in there.'"

I had to laugh, thinking of Em's quick wit. After a while, I put the urn in a crypt.

THE MOURNING DOVE STILL SINGS

A mid-June sun hangs warm and hazy
A woman hangs her laundry
In the gentle breeze
In between the trees
Her young son lays so lazy
In beams of fire
And puffs of velveteen
From above the evergreen

His daydream is soon disturbed
By the song of a sad, gray bird
And he wonders
Don't she have a home

And Mama said, that's the mourning dove
Grieving for all the long-lost sons
There's a love she holds for the ones
Who've gone away

And so her songs she'll always sing
For sons who've gone to memory
For they are still in mothers' hearts
While the mourning dove still sings

A thousand years have passed beneath me
and though it seems
I've taken the hard, dusty road
I drew the load

An open window stirs a memory
of beams of fire
and puffs of velveteen
From above the evergreen

And in a song, though filled with sadness
of long lost love, for me there's gladness
that still, I'm in my mother's heart
and the mourning dove still sings

Song lyrics by Emory
© 1990

Chapter Fifteen

A Sprig Sprouts

In 1992, we tied the knot. It was official! Shortly after we married, I got completely burned out with nursing. Paperwork had become more important than patients, and the rehab center was requiring more time than it was paying me for.

"Jay, I really don't want to continue with nursing. I wish I could find another job," I complained to him after a ten-hour day.

"Why don't you quit, then?" he asked me, providing a logical if not practical solution.

"And do what?" I countered.

"Start your own company," he said.

"My own company? What in the world can I possibly do to make any real money? I can do a little Amway business on the side, but it's not enough to quit my job. What would you suggest?"

"Just do something you know. Hey - I've got a good idea. Why don't you come to work with me?"

It sounded tempting, but I reminded him of the facts. "Because I'm gonna lose an income if I do that."

"No you won't. If you want to come work for me, I'll plan my estimates in such a way that I have an extra helper. That will be planned into the cost for the employer."

It worked out well after all. An added benefit was that I also had the option to take a day or two off if I needed to stay home. We were building decks, doing interior remodeling, basements, painting....

One thing driving my urge to get out of nursing was a serious problem with varicose veins. Years of being on my feet all day had exacerbated my condition to the point of terrible pain and protruding vessels. I thought helping Jay in construction would be easier, requiring less standing, but my circulation was getting worse and so was the pain. Finally I went to a doctor.

"We probably need to just strip these out. I'll give you the preparatory antibiotics, and next week we will do it."

"How long will I need to recover?" I inquired, dreading the thought of a long season being bed-bound.

"You'll be in one morning and I will send you home in the afternoon. In a few days, you can be on your feet four to six hours at a time as long as you wear heavy elastic hose for support."

"All right, then. It sounds good to me. I will be happy to be pain-free!"

The following Tuesday, I had fasted and taken the medications required. We got to the hospital at 5:00 a.m. The local anesthetic allowed me to be awake for the procedure. I watched the doctor make a two-inch incision at the top of each leg, just where it joins the torso to bend. Once inside, he stretched and tied some veins to others, and pulled out the offending varicosities. This offered smoother channels through which blood could flow.

After I spent some time in the recovery area where they gave me plenty of pain medication, they allowed Jay to take me home. Through the evening I was fine. I went to bed at around 10:00 p.m. Jay leaned over me.

"There, sweetheart," he smiled, sweet and gentle as he tucked me in. "If you need help in the night, don't hesitate to wake me. I'm right here for you." He brushed his teeth and joined me. In minutes he was fast asleep.

For me, drowsiness was precluded because the pain medicine was wearing off. My bladder felt full. *Maybe if I relieve myself, I will feel better. If not, I can take something while I'm up.* Ever the independent hero, I sat on the edge of the bed and then stood to my feet and hobbled to the toilet, only six yards from my side of the bed.

I sat down on the "throne" and pressed a little to eliminate my bladder. Without warning, dizziness overwhelmed me. *Uh-oh... I'd better get back to bed before I pass out.* In a less sedated state, I might have thought clearly enough to call Jay for help, but since I had not eaten and was full of drugs from the surgery, all I could think of was making it back to bed. I stood up.

In retrospect I know what happened. Days later I reexamined the event from a nurse's perspective and it made perfect sense. In the rectal area, there is a vegas nerve similar to the one that runs across the elbow. When pressure is put on it, pain occurs. As a nurse, when I had to digitally relieve patients of impaction, I was instructed to be extremely careful. Sudden pressure to the vegas nerve can create serious complications: even cessation of breathing.

As I stood, I had to walk around the tissue caddy between me and the door. I took three steps, but then stopped in helpless panic. I grabbed the caddy as an ice cold wave started at the top of my skull and poured itself through my body. In that instant, I knew I was dying. Everything went black. I died and then fell.

Jay heard a strange rattle that sat him upright in the bed, wide-awake. My hand had hit the window blind, startling him from deep sleep. In the glow of the nightlight, he saw my silhouette framed in the bathroom doorway. He watched briefly, noting that my shadow was becoming smaller and he knew I was falling, stiff as a two-by-four, backward. He became airborne in an attempt to get to me, but was a split-second too late. I hit, full force, from a standing position on the tile floor. He heard a death wheeze as he knelt and saw that my eyes had already rolled back in my head, showing only white. Touching me, he knew I was dead. His police experience had taught him CPR, and he started immediately. Soon he had me breathing. Racing down the hall to the kitchen, he called 9-1-1 and then hurried back to be sure I was still alive. He said I kept breathing until the paramedics arrived, but then stopped a few more times during the ambulance ride to North Fulton Hospital, requiring more resuscitation.

Jay was convinced the only thing allowing him to revive me was a long-shag throw rug in front of the bathroom sink. My head hit there. Had I been one inch in either direction, I would have hit the toilet or the bare floor. I am sure the rug helped, but I know now the reason I was allowed to resume life: God had other plans for me.

I spent two days in intensive care and three more in the progressive unit with a fractured skull. The doctor was amazed.

"The pressure of the blood that coagulated around her brain should have killed her," he noted. It took a few days for my memory to recover. Jay would visit; I could recognize him but not remember his name.

Visitors came to see me and when they left, I'd ask the nurse who they were. Slowly, though, my bruised brain healed, leaving me only a slight problem with balance. When I descend stairs, I can't bend my head enough to see where to put my feet without becoming dizzy. That need for help is just a reminder to me of the One who gave me my life back.

Three days into my stay, a nurse came to help me with a bath. As we completed the process, I asked her if I could put on some lipstick "to look nice when my husband comes."

"Of course, honey," she said, pulling up the mirror attached to the dinner tray and handing it to me. Looking into it, I screamed! Tears streamed down my face as I wept, not recognizing the monster staring back from the glass. Because of the blow to the back of my head, blood had been pushed forward and had collected in my face. Raccoon eyes, black into my cheeks, made me look like a character from a horror movie. I laugh thinking back on it because days later, a social worker came in to investigate my injury. She suspected I was a battered wife.

Miraculously, I recovered, and after a while went back into the renovation business with Jay. It was during one such job that the thing-a-ma-bob surfaced again in our thinking. We were working on a deck for a man named Gary who lived in Country Club of the South. One day as we were working, I noticed a little decorative fish head on the downspout for Gary's outside drain.

"Look at that, Jay. Isn't that cute?" I said, pointing out the fish.

"Yeah, it is. Gary said he invented that, patented it, and then Home Depot did the marketing. He's made a fortune off that little 'trout spout.'"

"Oh really? Gary invented it? And Gary got it patented? And Gary lives in Country Club of the South? Hmmm... Well Gary is the guy we need to talk with!"

Jay eyed me suspiciously. "Now what are you thinking?" he asked, standing up and concentrating on my face.

"About the thing-a-ma-bob."

"No, I'm not gonna bother him with that," he said, and knelt to grab his hammer.

"Well, fine. I am!" I told him.

"Don't you dare..." he scolded. But I was determined. This was a good project, and Gary might just be the one to help us get it done! When he came home for lunch that day, I called him.

"Gary, can you come here for a minute? I want to talk to you." He stepped to the door of the kitchen and invited us in.

"That deck is looking great," he said as we came into the room. "What's up?" I explained to him about Jay's frustration and the invention that was born of it.

"I'd like for you to just look at this thing and tell us what you think. It would only take a minute to check it out," I insisted.

"Sure, you bet! I'd be glad to evaluate it." He seemed genuinely interested.

"Great! I'll bring it tomorrow." The next morning, I laid a copy of the drawing on his dining table, and we worked all day on the deck. Gary didn't come home for lunch that afternoon, but as we walked in the door at home later that day, the phone was ringing. I answered.

"Hi Nikki, this is Gary. Let me talk to Jay," he said, and I handed him the phone. Jay listened a moment, and then responded.

"Nope, there's nothing like that out there, 'cause if there was, I'd have found it - believe me!" Another pause. "Well, yeah; I have the original plans with the notary seal on them. Sure, you can keep those for a while."

Two weeks went by, and we finished Gary's job. He called the following Monday.

"Jay, I want to get a patent on this because I want to protect you. I've talked to a couple of people I know at Home Depot, and they said I should get it patented and then come back and talk with them. If I haven't missed something and what you're telling me is true, we can easily get it done. If it already exists, they won't give us the patent."

The little tool flew through the patent search, and Gary called again.

"Man," he said, "I'm excited! I think we've got something here. We're both gonna make some money. I'll tell you what I'm willing to do: I'll front all the money if you're willing to give me fifty percent of the net profit. I don't even care about getting my money back initially; I will just take it out of my share. I'm making money; I don't care."

"That's a deal! You put it together, hire a lawyer and get the patent. If you're willing to do that, I'll certainly share the profits with you."

It was out of our hands and into Gary's. Again, it went to the back burner of our consciousness.

Whatever job came up, we would go offer an estimate. The more experience I garnered, the more I realized that if this business was going to grow and make any real money, we needed somebody else in the seat, on the phone doing the executive work.

"I need time to be able to get information. I need to be able to plan how to build a company," I told Jay.

"Well, I don't want us to get too big," he answered.

"I know, baby, but we need to be bigger than this if we're gonna have a decent income and plan a retirement. We can't just go on this way; we're not getting any younger!"

Finally he agreed. I broke away from the hands-on labor and opened the construction office. With the help of volunteers at the Small Business Administration, I got lots of information about operating a company. I went to their downtown headquarters and did extensive research. I called and asked hundreds of questions, and in a matter of time, I built our construction company into a multi-million dollar enterprise. We started doing huge projects. I went to prestigious Buckhead and bought a piece of property just six houses away from the Governor's mansion. We tore down the old home and built a 2.5 million-dollar mansion on the gorgeous lot. Jay was the field engineer who ran the job. All was going well. We were earning a six-figure income. I started investing it, putting money back into the company to make it grow. But as it grew and resources poured in, our personal lives began to crumble. Insufficient sleep made it easy for us to snap at each other. Social engagements and meetings with clients encouraged increased alcohol consumption. We were arguing more often than we were conversing.

One day not long after the marital struggles began, I was minding my own business, shopping in the local supermarket when the unbelievable happened. I rounded the corner of the canned goods aisle and ran right into my old nemesis! As shocked as I was, Lydia offered a wide smile and said, "Well, hello! Long time no see."

Something was different. I wasn't offended by her and didn't bristle at her greeting. In fact, we stood there and talked for more than ten minutes. She told me about the birth of her second son, and I told her about Em's death. Tears came into her eyes and she hugged me.

"I'm so sorry," she said, looking right into my face. There was a genuine tenderness I hadn't noticed in her before. "You know," she said, "we wasted a lot of time when we could have been friends. I'd like to start over. Do you think the four of us could get together for dinner soon?"

"I'd like that," I told her, surprised at the openness of our conversation. "I could use a friend right now. I'll talk to Jay and call you." We exchanged phone numbers and parted to finish our shopping.

The following week, we met for dinner. I found out they had quit Amway and had moved to East Cobb, not far from us. Lydia had gone through a personal crisis and had come out of it a more tender and empathetic person. She talked about a relationship with God, and I could tell He had made a difference in her life. Instead of the self-righteous, perfectionistic prude I had detested, I found in this new Lydia a compassionate confidante and a true friend.

With business pressures, Jay's drinking increased. He was argumentative most of the time. He wasted money taking guys to lunch and treating them in bars. We argued about what he was spending. Then I started drinking, and our arguments escalated into physical fights. That's when he started flirting with Louise. She was the real estate agent who had sold me the property. She had Jay come do some remodeling in her house, and I found out he was taking her to lunch and to dinner once in a while. One night I confronted him.

"Just why is it that you're spending so much time with Louise?" I challenged him when he came in after 11 p.m.

"Well," he said flatly, "when I come home, you and I are fighting. When I go and sit in her house for a drink or stand on her back porch having a cigarette, we aren't fighting. The air is just more breathable over there."

I knew he was telling the truth, but I still didn't like it.

"Are you sleeping with her?"

"Believe it or not, I just enjoy some adult conversation without being nagged and accused," he snapped back.

"Well, I think you just need to pack your crap and get out of my house. Go there, to Louise. That's where you want to be anyway," I told him.

In my twisted way of thinking, I really expected him to apologize and promise me he'd stop seeing her. My manipulation didn't work. He packed his bags and left. The next day he was back, but it didn't last long. Two weeks of drinking, bickering and fighting finally escalated to an unbearable level. We'd been together for thirteen years, married for six, when Jay decided he'd had enough. On Valentine's Day, 1999, after a horrible verbal battle, he grabbed me by the throat and shoved me onto the couch. I was relieved when he left. I'd lost my soul mate and with him, everything that meant life to me.

About a month after he left, I learned I had a small tumor in my right breast. A lumpectomy verified it was malignant. That Friday I went home from surgery, alone, afraid and depressed. Two days later, on Sunday, while I was still in the throes of the terrifying news, Jay walked in the kitchen door. He didn't ask me how I was doing or what was new in my life. We hadn't seen each other for several weeks. He walked in with a strange smile on his face.

"Nikki, I brought you these papers to sign. It shouldn't take long, and I'll be on my way." He didn't look at my face. I was frozen in the doorway.

"What papers are those?" I asked him, as if I didn't know.

"Divorce papers. I need your signature, and then we can get this over with," he said in a businesslike voice.

For a moment I was too stunned to speak. Here he was, my heart and soul, the man I had loved at first sight and ever since. We had been married to each other, and now he wanted me to sign papers and send him away?

"You know what, you're gonna burn in hell before I'll sign those papers. Forget it. Take your papers and get out of here. You're not getting a divorce." I turned and left the room so he wouldn't see the tears spilling down my cheeks. Moments later, I heard the kitchen door shut. I peeked out the window and saw his truck pull from the driveway and down the street.

By this time, I had realized that my tendency toward addiction was making me an alcoholic. I joined a self-help group, but my willpower wasn't strong enough. With Jay gone and the summer dying into autumn, my last glimmer of hope flickered out. I'd eaten nothing for three days, but a bottle was always in my hand. I knew I was slowly torturing myself to death, but I didn't really care. In early August, with nowhere else to turn, I called my friend. It rang several times, and I expected the answering machine any second when a familiar voice spoke into my ear.

"Hello, this is Lydia," she said.

"Lydia, this is Nikki," I choked. My voice broke. "Lydia..." I began to sob and couldn't make sense to her on the phone. "Can you come over?" I finally said.

"Sure. I will be there in twenty minutes. You just stay where you are, okay?" She must have known I was in trouble because she didn't waste any time. It was early afternoon when she arrived. I don't think it took her twenty minutes. I know I looked frightful when she came in. My "liquid diet" had dropped eight pounds from my already thin frame and my cheeks were hollow from dehydration. I was barely wearing my bathrobe. My hair was disheveled. My puffy, tear-stained face needed washing. Lydia knocked, and I heard her try the knob.

"Nikki?" she called as she came in through the unlocked door.

"In the living room," I replied without getting up. She frowned when she saw me and hurried to my chair to give me a hug.

"You poor thing," she said. "What happened?" I explained to her about our fighting, the separation and his visit to serve the papers.

"You know, I run into Jay at the gas station once in a while when each of us passes through going to work. In fact, one day when I went in, the attendant asked me about him, thinking we were related or something. When I saw him a couple of days ago, he just looked at the ground, so I asked him what was wrong. He told me you guys had separated, and I couldn't believe it. He told me you were hard to live with, but because of his body language, I thought he wasn't telling me the whole story. Nikki, I am so sorry." She sat on the footstool beside my chair and held my hand quietly for a few minutes. Then she fished into her handbag and passed me a Kleenex.

"I'm going to make some coffee and toast. You need to eat something."

She busied herself in the kitchen and came back in a few minutes with strong, black coffee, toast and jam on a tray. She sipped coffee and we talked while

I downed the food she offered. By that time, it was dusk.

"I have a rehearsal for a performance at church," she said when I'd finished my snack. "Are you going to be all right?"

"I think so. I really appreciate you coming," I told her, managing a smile. "I think I'll take a shower and go to bed."

"That's a good idea. I'll call you tomorrow," Lydia promised.

I did take a shower, but as I sobered, the pain came back with all the self-doubt, the accusations, the regrets, the hopelessness... I went to find my bottle to drown the voices in my head. After a few swigs, I felt better. To be more accurate, I should say I felt nothing. I slumped into the chair where Lydia had left me and thought about tomorrow. She'd said she'd call. *What if I'm not here? Why don't I just end it tonight and not trouble her any more?* Alcohol and all of its associated demons were driving my thoughts. I got up and found my gun. No matter how drunk I became, I always knew where the gun was, and I remembered how to use it. *I'll just call Lydia and say goodbye. She was so kind to come today...* I laid the pistol on the side table and dialed her number. John answered.

"Is Lydia there?" I slurred.

"Nikki?"

"Yeah, it's me," I said. "Look, could you tell Lydia goodbye for me? She won't need to come tomorrow," I told him.

"Nikki, are you okay?" he wanted to know.

"I don't know, John. I'm drunk. I think that's about the best option at this point," I said.

"Look, I'm coming over. I need to talk to you. Just wait for me to get there, okay? Will you promise?"

I promised him I'd wait for him. I wondered what he wanted to talk to me about, what was so urgent. Was something wrong with Lydia? We hung up. I slumped into my chair, and sleep overtook me. I didn't hear John come in, but he woke me with a cup of strong, black coffee.

"There you are," he said quietly, putting it on the table beside me. The gun was gone.

"You said you wanted to talk to me? Is Lydia okay? Why didn't she come with you?" I sipped the coffee and my speech became more lucid.

"She's at a rehearsal. She's fine. But she came by the house after she left here and told me she was really worried about you. We've been praying for you. She told me you might need some company tonight. Look, Nikki, I know you are in a severe depression and that you've been living on alcohol. You can't go on like this. Will you let me take you to a hospital and get you the help you need?"

His eyes were kind and his voice gentle. I knew he was sincere. Tears streamed down my face.

"You're right, John," I admitted, sniffling. "I was ready to die, in fact, was planning on it tonight. You and Lydia saved my life. I'll do whatever you think necessary."

He took me to Charter-Peachford, and I stayed for over a week. They fed me, weaned me off the liquor and put me on a sedative. Lydia and her children came to visit, and they brought me flowers and pictures they'd drawn. I was loved. There was something to live for after all.

Lydia came to get me at the end of my stay. We pulled into my driveway and I sat, transfixed, inside the safety of my seatbelt.

"I can't go in there," I told her.

"Why not? Is it the memories?" she asked.

"I don't know what it is, but I just get chills and feel afraid when I'm in the house. I know that sounds crazy..."

"No, it doesn't." She was looking at me with concern. "I think we need to go inside, pray in every room of your house, and command any evil spirits living in there to leave!" That sounded a little bizarre to me, but if it would help, I was willing to go along.

We got out of the car and went to the porch. I handed Lydia the key. She opened the door and laid her hand on the doorframe.

"Have you got any oil?"

"Yeah, there's some corn oil in the kitchen," I said. She went in that direction.

"In the cabinet next to the stove," I called after her.

She came back with the bottle. She poured a little into her hand and set the bottle on the floor. Then she dipped two fingers into the oil she'd poured in her left palm and smeared it across the doorframe.

"In the name of Jesus, we claim this house for God. We command that you, Satan, and your demons of suicide, depression, anger, rage, fear and bitterness leave this place. This house is under the blood of Jesus Christ, and you have no authority here any more. Leave and don't come back. Thank you, Lord Jesus Christ, for your blood that is able to free Nikki and her home from all of these evil things."

We went in and she closed the front door. She went through the entire place, anointing every passageway and praying something similar in every room. When we finished the ritual cleansing, she called me to the couch.

"Now, Nikki, you don't need to be afraid of anything living in this house. What you need to do at this point is to ask the Lord to be your personal Savior. You need to come to Jesus."

"How do I do that?" I asked her, desperate to have the kind of peace I'd seen in her.

"You need to admit you are helpless, that you can't even live on your own. Realize that Jesus Christ offers you new life, hope and peace. You can't find that in a bottle or anywhere else you've looked."

I thought about my life to this point, and I knew she was absolutely right.

"You need to tell Jesus you believe in Him and want Him to be your Savior and your friend. He's promised to do that if we just ask. Do you want that?"

"Yes, very much," I told her.

"Okay. I'll lead you in a prayer. Just repeat after me and mean it from your heart."

As I prayed after Lydia, coming to God like a young child, I could feel peace washing through my soul. As I told God I was a sinner and admitted I needed His help, I knew in my heart He was listening, forgiving me for all the garbage in my life, bathing me in the blood of Christ and making a new person out of me. It was the first time I'd felt like someone knew all the junk in my life and loved me anyway. I was free!

When we finished, we were quiet for a while. I realized my face was wet, but this time they were not tears of anger or self-pity but of joy.

"Now Nikki, this is your first day with Jesus, and you will never go back. Your life will be different, starting today. Jesus Christ has given you a clean slate: a fresh, new start."

She was right. That old Nikki was gone forever. I was about to begin an adventure that even in my wildest dreams, I couldn't have imagined.

Chapter Sixteen

Tilling Fallow Ground

With Jay gone, my construction business had no employees. Without a steady income, I needed a job. Nursing was out of the question; I had been diagnosed with rheumatoid arthritis while Jay and I were still together, and the lifting required of nurses was no longer an option for me. I decided to go back to being a waitress, and I got a job at Waffle House.

The restaurant was near my home, although not close enough to walk. I enjoyed the interaction with people, and they often told me their woes, which helped me keep my own in perspective. As Lydia had explained, my viewpoint was different now. I talked about my new faith with anyone who would listen and tried to remember the people who talked to me each day and pray for them. It was while in such a mindset that I met Dennis.

He was nineteen, almost young enough to be my grandchild, when he came to work with us in the kitchen on my shift. Between customers, he told me about having a fight with his parents and leaving home with no intent of returning.

"What was it about?"

"Whatever it's always about. My step-dad drinks like a fish, and when he gets drunk, he starts whacking at whatever moves. I've had more black eyes and bruises than I can count. Last Thursday was it for me. I'm legally old enough to leave, and I don't have to put up with his crap."

Boy, did that sound familiar! I thought of the many times I had climbed out the window, of the marriage at fifteen to get away from home, of my mother's choosing Tony over me...

"Where are you staying?" I asked him.

"I'd been sleeping in a friend's car until his folks got wind of it. They hit the roof, and he told me I'd have to find another place," he said.

My heart broke for him. What would I do in his shoes? What would Jesus do in mine?

"You know, Dennis, I have a three-bedroom house with two bathrooms. Why don't you come to my place until you find something else? You can help me with the yard in exchange. Since we work the same shift, we can ride together," I offered.

"Wow - do you mean it? That would be super. It would be nice to sleep in a bed again," he admitted.

That night after we got off at 11:00, he tossed his duffel bag into my back seat, and we headed for home.

During our shift, a kind gentleman named Tom stopped in regularly for coffee. He always sat in the same place, and I was his waitress. When business was slow, he would invite me to have a cup with him, and we'd talk about many things. On the second night of Dennis' stay, I let him take the car home so he could sleep. He was coming at the end of my shift to get me and then planned to work a double himself. However, when 10:55 came and there was no Dennis, I started to worry. I knew he turned the phones off while he was sleeping, so there was no chance of waking him. Tom was in his regular booth, getting ready to leave.

"Tom, I wonder if I could ask you a big favor? I let Dennis take my car, and evidently he's overslept. Would you mind hanging out a few more minutes and giving me a ride home?"

"Absolutely. I'd be glad to," he responded, smiling.

When Dennis didn't show up at 11:10, Tom chauffeured me home. To my great surprise, though, the house was dark. The car was still in the driveway, but Dennis didn't answer the doorbell. He wasn't there.

"Oh, brother," I dug through my purse and then looked up at Tom. "I gave him my car keys, and the one to the house is on the same ring."

Tom went to his car for a flashlight and then cased the house like a burglar.

"Do you have a window open anywhere?" he asked.

"No, I don't leave anything cracked," I lamented. For once I regretted being so efficient.

"Is your house door unlocked inside the garage?"

"Yeah, it is."

"Then why don't I break a small window in the garage door? It will be cheaper to replace than the larger ones on the house," he suggested. "With that out, I can reach through, open the garage door, and we can get in."

"That sounds like a plan," I answered, amazed at his logical thinking. He proceeded to wrap his hand with an extra towel he kept for checking the oil in his car. Then he punched through the pane closest to the handle. In moments, the door was up, and we were inside. I wasn't sure what had gone on, so Tom came in with me while I turned on all the lights and checked the house.

"You've been so nice to bring me home and then help me get in. Why don't you stay for a while? I'll put on some coffee, and we can chat."

He accepted my offer, and I made the coffee. There was no sign of Dennis; I wasn't sure whether to expect him or not, and I knew he had my keys. Another person in the house was comforting at this point, and Tom said he didn't have anything else to do. We talked for thirty minutes or more about our families. He told me about his mother, who lived in a neighboring county. He was visiting her twice a month on weekends to spend the day, take her to lunch and errands, do yard work and other "guy" stuff.

"That is the sign of a good son," I said, "one who takes care of his aging mom."

"Well, I figure it is part of my responsibility as a Christian, not only because I'm her son. I'm really thankful to have a mom like her," he returned. "Let me ask you something, Nikki. If Jesus walked in that door right now, what would you say to Him? What would you tell Him you're thankful for?"

"I'd hardly know where to begin, Tom. He's really been good to me. I just came to Christ about four months ago. I was at the point of suicide, but now life is very different. Every day I find new things to be grateful for. How long have you been a Christian?" I asked him.

He explained to me that he'd spent most of his adult years as a believer, and that he'd attended a large Christian university where he'd studied Bible courses. We had a wonderful time of fellowship then, talking about Jesus and how He'd changed our lives. Before we knew it, it was after 1 a.m.

"I'd better get home. I have to work tomorrow," he said.

"I'm sorry to keep you out so late. I really don't think Dennis is coming back tonight. Do you have to get up early?"

"No, I'm doing a second tomorrow. I work swing-shifts," he added.

He explained he was a security supervisor at the CDC in downtown Atlanta. I saw him to the door, and we said goodbye. I went to the bedroom and flipped on the light. There were my keys on the bathroom vanity with a note from Dennis.

Dear Nikki,

Thanks for your help. Sorry I had to run without a real 'goodbye.' My brother came in from Florida and called me on my cell. I've gone with him. Here are your keys. You're a terrific lady. Dennis

I smiled at the teenaged enthusiasm that had taken my young friend out of my life and locked me out of my own house. *I'm glad he's with his family. Lord, will you send somebody else to love Dennis and help him see You?*

Over the next few months, Tom and I became good friends. He took me to lunch and to dinner a few times, and he continued to be a regular at Waffle House. However, our friendship was simply that. Romance was never involved; Tom was like a brother to me, and without my realizing it, he was discipling me in my fledgling faith. Sometime in September after my first birthday as a Christian, Tom told me his landlord needed the property where he was living and he asked me if I knew of anything nearby to rent.

"Why don't you rent my extra bedroom?" I asked him. "I am struggling to make ends meet and could use the financial help. I know I can trust you and would love to help by providing a good place for you to live."

He thought about it for a week and then agreed to an October move-in date.

Tom and I lived our separate lives, but often had conversations about our faith. He taught me many things from the Bible and explained to me methods of personal devotion that would help me feed myself from the Word. He prayed with me at times, and from his example I learned I could talk to God about mundane, daily things as well as big issues. As I think back over my life, I realize that God also used Tom to teach me a more general lesson: not all men are like locusts, waiting to devour. In most cases, God uses more mature Christian ladies to teach women younger in their faith. Throughout my life, my protector, provider and then predator had always been a man. I see now that God brought Tom to my life to help restore my trust; a man under the headship of Jesus Christ was much different than other men not under His influence.

By the time Tom took up residence, I had changed jobs and was working for BP, a gas station and convenience store. Like the Waffle House, it was near home, but the hours were better and the work environment much more congenial. That fall, however, my health rapidly deteriorated. Arthritis was keeping me at some level of consistent discomfort.

One unforgettable January night, I was standing behind the counter at the store when my knees buckled, and I collapsed to the floor in excruciating pain. It was almost 10 p.m., and though my replacement was due, she was usually late. I couldn't stand. I dragged myself to the place where I could reach my purse on the floor behind the counter and dug out my cell phone. *Calling home is futile,* I told myself. *You know Tom is never there on a Friday night! It's his only night off. Why should he be home?* It rang four

times and the answering machine picked up. Hoping
against hope, I left a message: "Tom, if you're there,
I need your help! I'm on the floor at work and I can't
get up. There's nobody else here. Please call my cell.
Thanks."

I was lying there praying, still in unbearable pain,
when I heard the door open. Mercifully in the few
minute interim, no customers had come in. Peering
between the counter and the walk-through gate, I
saw my replacement. She was on time! Right behind
her, in walked Tom, his face etched with worry.

"Nikki?" he called as he approached the counter.

"Here, Tom, on the floor," I moaned. He hurried
through the gate and helped me into the office chair
by the cash register.

"What happened?" he wanted to know. I was still
in pain and told him I couldn't talk about it now.

"Could you please just get me home?" He stuffed
my phone into my handbag and set it in my lap. I
grimaced, then cried out when we hit a bump as he
pushed me to the car in the wheeled office chair.

"Can you drive?" he asked as he opened my car
door.

"I think so," I managed, and got the keys from
my purse.

"I'll follow you home," he decided, and went to
his vehicle. When we pulled into the driveway, he
was at my door as soon as I opened it.

"Wait," he said. "Let me help you." He slid one
arm under my knees and the other behind my back
and lifted me, giving the door a gentle prod with his
foot to close it. Then he carried me into my bedroom

and set me on the bed. My face was wet with tears, and I was still in severe pain. Tom knelt in front of me and looked into my eyes.

"I'm not sure what to do. Maybe I should get you to the hospital," he wondered aloud.

"No! Just help me get into bed and then let me rest. I hurt too much to go anywhere. Please..." I begged him, pain shooting through my back and into my legs.

Tom was a little older than me and quite a gentleman. God gave him grace that night to be my male nurse. Poor Tom, apologizing the whole time, tried to make me comfortable. He undressed me, tenderly unzipping and lifting my blouse, fidgeting loose the hooks of my bra and removing it, then handing me the sheet to cover myself, pulling my slacks from my legs...Never was there the slightest hint of impropriety. Tom's whole attention was on meeting my need. During this entire process, I screamed and cried intermittently. In all my life, I'd never had such unrelenting pain.

"I still think I should call the hospital. We don't know what this is," he said softly.

"No... no! I know you're just trying to help, and I am thankful, but now just please go away and leave me alone."

The next morning, I called the rheumatologist and told him what happened. He agreed to see me, and Tom drove me to the office. The doctor gave me a series of shots, but warned that it could take 24 to 48 hours before I'd notice a difference. The shots never offered relief. Three days later, the pain was still the same.

For nine days, I didn't leave the bedroom. When I had to go to the bathroom, Tom would help me, pushing me in a chair with wheels or carrying me. When he had to go to work, I couldn't function. I lay in the bed, catching catnaps between stabs of pain.

On the ninth day, I called my church. The receptionist answered.

"Hello. I was wondering if I could talk to the pastor," I told her.

"Well, sure, you can do that. But can I find out... What is the nature of your call? Should I tell him you need to speak to him about a personal issue?"

"Yes, I am really just not well right now, and I'd like to talk to him about that."

"Okay, then. I don't think he's at his desk, but is it all right if I put you into his voice mail? He will call you back."

"Sure," I told her. I explained into the machine that I was having some health issues and asked if he'd talk with me about it. I left him my phone number and my name and hung up. Within the hour, he called back. He listened kindly as I detailed my situation.

"I don't know whether the church believes in healing and that kind of thing because I am a new Christian and don't know all the church teaches. But I do understand that the Scriptures are very clear about when we are ill, we are to go to the elders and pray for healing, and that we should be anointed. I'm not entirely clear on this, but if you don't mind, I'd like to be prayed for and anointed."

"Oh, Nikki, by all means," he said, encouraging me. "We would like very much to do that with you. I'll tell you what: we're having a board meeting on Monday night, and the elders will be there. Could you come then? Let's set up an appointment. We'll be happy to anoint you and pray with you."

I was to be there at 7:00. This was Friday; Monday was not far away. In the midst of my pain, I was filled with hope and anticipation.

The next morning, Tom was scheduled to visit his mother. As he was preparing to leave, he came to the door of my room.

"What can I do for you before I go?" he asked with a kind smile.

"You know, I'd really love to just go out and lie on the sofa and spend the whole day nibbling and watching TV. I'd just like to get out of this bed."

He helped me out to the living room, set a tray beside the couch with snacks, a pitcher of water and other things I might want. He also put my cell phone there in case I needed to call a neighbor to help me. Extra pillows and another blanket were the final additions. He stacked them on the floor beside me.

"Can you think of anything else?" he asked, patting my hand.

"No, my friend. I think you've got it covered! Go and have a great day with your mom. Thanks for everything."

"Oh," he said, turning back to the hallway. In a moment he returned with my Bible.

"You might want this," he commented, handing it to me. Then he said goodbye and went out.

I picked up the remote and turned on the TV. I surfed the channels until I came to a religious station. An evangelist was preaching, so I picked up my Bible and followed his message. It was interesting and inspirational at the time, but it didn't make a lasting enough impression for me to long remember his topic. After the teaching time was finished, though, he walked through the audience, allowing people to stand if they would like prayer. I watched as he prayed for a woman who had recently lost her baby. Then an older man asked him to pray for a new housing situation for him. Another man asked him to pray for healing of his mother, a cancer patient.

Although the message didn't stick, I will never forget what happened next. He looked straight into the camera – right into my eyes – and said, "The Lord has just told me I need to pray with someone who's watching us, who is having severe low back pain and can barely walk. You are looking to God for healing, and I just want to pray with you right now. I know you're a long distance away from me, but just reach your hand out as a point of connection, and I'm going to pray with you. God is healing you right now."

I knew he was talking to me! Perhaps he spoke to a hundred other people also, but at that moment, I agreed with his prayer and knew that God had chosen to begin His healing work in me. As he prayed, I didn't feel hot flashes, see lightening or even have tingles, but I had absolutely the most wonderful, warm, peaceful assurance I have ever known. Inside, the precious voice of Jesus said to me, "Stand up and walk. I am with you here, and it's going to be okay."

For the first time in ten days, I swung my legs over the edge of the couch and slowly stood on my own two feet, totally pain free! For three weeks I had not known a moment without pain, even before the collapse, and here I was: standing, then walking across the room without any discomfort at all. I was so excited and happy, I had to tell someone. I called my mother. I called all the people I could remember who had been praying for me to tell them God had begun my healing!

I can't say I remained pain-free for the entire weekend, but from that moment, I certainly improved. On Monday night, I drove myself to the church and walked in using only one cane. I entered the building to find our pastor waiting for me.

"Hi there," he greeted. "I'm glad you're here." I met him as quickly as I could, grinning from ear to ear.

"I have to tell you," I began, "God started the work this weekend, and I've come so He can finish it!"

He escorted me into the room, and I sat down. I recognized a few of the faces of the men around the table, but some were strangers to me. They asked questions, getting to know me and my situation. I told them how I had come to Jesus and what my experience with the Lord had taught me this far. They were so interested and compassionate toward me; I truly felt the presence of the Holy Spirit among us. After we had talked for a while, one of the men picked up a small bottle of oil, and the group gathered around me. Someone poured a little oil on my head. The men laid their hands on my back, shoulders and arms as I sat in the chair and they surrounded me. One at a time, they prayed. I felt Jesus' hands among theirs as they spoke to Him. I knew He was touching me and was doing the work that only He could do.

After the meeting, I had no pain. I could walk and move as I had done a month before. The next day, I told anyone who would listen about what God had done for me. I went back to work full time and had no trouble at all. I thought everyone who had been involved in my miracle would be just as excited as I was about it. God had showed off in my life, and I wanted to make sure everyone gave Him the praise He deserved for such a marvelous deed.

On Sunday, I saw the pastor when I entered the sanctuary. He was talking to someone. Since he was on the other side of the church from me, I decided to literally skip and run to him to demonstrate what God had done. He had finished his conversation, so he turned and smiled when he saw me.

"Look, Pastor. Look what God did! Look what He's done for me – isn't it wonderful?" I spun in a circle like a child who'd just won a fabulous prize.

"Isn't that nice?" he commented, and he turned to greet someone else.

I was stunned. I hoped I had misunderstood what I perceived as indifference. But in the days that followed, no mention was made of my healing. No opportunity was offered for me to share my experience or give a testimony. Not one of the elders who had prayed for me followed up to find out what God had done. To say I was disappointed would be a grave understatement. I was embarrassed - grieved - that our church family had so little gratitude to offer back to the God of Miracles who had worked in my life. Our Heavenly Father gave our church that gift for a reason, and we didn't even bother to unwrap it.

The summer went by with Jay and me in and out of court. He was insisting I sign divorce papers, and I consistently refused. I didn't want a divorce. Again and again, the decision was postponed. In October, the judge who had been handling our case died, and a new justice assumed the bench. I was notified of yet another hearing. This new magistrate was clearing the books.

"What part of 'I don't want a divorce' do you not understand?" I asked my lawyer.

"Well, Nikki, if Jay doesn't show up, you may get it anyway whether you like it or not!" he told me.

"No. I don't have to have it if I don't want it. I want you to have him throw it out. I don't want a divorce."

The night before the hearing, I had gone on the website for the Praise Team at church and asked them to pray with me that the judge would not grant the divorce. They'd assured me they were praying, and I knew they were standing with me.

That morning, my lawyer and I found ourselves in the courtroom without opposition. The new judge looked at us and asked me many questions. With tears streaming down my face, I answered the best I could. Through choking sobs, I told him, "I don't want this divorce," but the judge wasn't even listening to me! He looked at my lawyer.

"Is everything in place the way you want it?" the robed tyrant queried.

"Yes, Your Honor." My attorney betrayed me.

"Divorce granted," the hard-hearted judge announced. "Next case," he said, waving us from his presence.

"No!" I shouted. "What just happened here?" I cried aloud.

The lawyer grabbed my arm.

"Come on, Nikki," he said. "We're out of here," he said, and ushered me out of the courtroom. In the hallway, he stopped and glared at me. "How long are you going to beat a dead horse? The man doesn't want you. He doesn't want this marriage. It's over."

I drove home by myself, but I knew I wasn't alone. Through hot tears, I told the Lord, "You still have a plan for my life, and I have to trust that You know what you're doing in all of this. I'm just gonna move forward."

I felt empty, like a fallow field. Maybe God was plowing me to plant something new. I didn't dare to wonder what crop He had in mind.

Chapter Seventeen

The Fog Clears

Fast forward seven months to a sunny Sunday afternoon in May, 2003. I was at Lydia's, helping her prepare for a graduation party for her oldest son.

"Nikki, does this look all right?" Lydia called from the dining room. I poked my head through the kitchen door. She was twisting maroon and gold streamers together.

"Oh, yeah. That will be festive," I assured her, and went back to the sink to finish washing some fruit.

"Where did you put those serving platters and bowls I brought from the house?" I called to her.

"You know, I was looking for them last night. Are you sure they got into your car with the other stuff? I never could find them."

I stopped washing and stared out the window, thinking. I couldn't remember putting them in the car.

"Lydia, you're right," I dried my hands and joined her in the next room. "I made a note to myself, but I can't picture gathering them into a stack or transferring them to the car. Do you think I have time to run to the house and get them?"

"Oh, yeah," she smiled. "It's another couple of hours before the kids get here. Anyway, if we're still putting out food when they trickle in, they won't care. I think we're gonna need that stuff, the platters especially," she reminded me. "And what about those spiral sandwiches that were in your freezer?"

"Probably still there. Okay then, I'll be back soon," I told her. "I think I'll change into more comfortable shoes while I'm there, too. These heels are good for church, but standing all afternoon and trying to smile may be a different story."

"All right. See you in a bit. I'll call if we need anything else," she said as I found my purse and left the room.

I had made it a habit whenever I returned home to check the answering machine. Sure enough, it was blinking. I picked up the phone and hit the button.

"Hey, it's me!" a familiar voice said. "I'm trying to call you. Give me a ring back at this number please."

My heart beat a little harder. I wasn't sure if it was anger, disgust, fear or vengeance. *He's got a lot of nerve. First he wants a divorce, then he wants me to call him. Fat chance of that!* I pressed the erase button, and Jay's request vanished. The second message came up. The machine told me the call had come about ten minutes after the first one.

"Hey. It's me. I don't know if you got my first message, but if you did, please return my call. If you didn't get it, well... okay. But when you get this one, please call me. I need to talk to you."

Without hesitation, I erased it. I went to the bedroom and found a pair of pants and a jersey knit shirt. Before I could button it, the phone rang. I assumed it was Lydia, telling me she forgot something, so I went to check the caller ID. It was Jay. I stood by the receiver, frozen, debating with myself. *I have to get back to Sissy's... She's trying to have this party, and is depending on me. I don't have time to talk to him. Anyway, why should I?* It stopped ringing, and I breathed a sigh of relief. Five minutes elapsed during which time I gathered the necessary dishes. I had the car keys in hand, ready to walk out the door when the phone rang again. *Man, this is getting ridiculous!* I carefully laid my parcels on the couch and walked across the room, but by the time I got to it, the answering machine had kicked in. I waited while he left the message, then picked it up.

"Nik, please... PLEASE answer my calls. I have to talk to you. It's urgent. Please... I desperately need to speak to you."

My heart ached. *My gosh! What if something's wrong? At least I'll return the call and be sure he's all right.* The phone only rang once on the other end.

"Hello."

"Jay? Are you all right?"

"Gosh, do you know I've been trying to call you all day?" he queried.

"You know, I didn't call for you to chastise me. What do you need? Are you okay?"

"Yeah, I'm fine. Why?"

"Well, your calls were so urgent, and I'm busy right now. I don't have time to talk. Can I call you back later?"

"No," he answered.

"What do you mean, 'no'? I'm busy right now," I told him, getting a little irritated.

"Look," he replied, "I won't keep you. Just answer a question for me. Will you meet me later for dinner?"

"*What*?" I was speechless.

"Will you meet me later and have dinner? I need to talk to you."

"Jay, listen. I'm not going through any more crap with you. We've been there, done all that... This is not working! Every time we meet, we end up in a bad mood, and one of us gets angry. I just don't want to go through -"

"Nikki," he interrupted, "just shut up and listen to me. It isn't about that. I just need to talk to you. Will you give me some time? Will you sit down over dinner and talk to me?"

"Can I think about it?" My head was spinning.

"All right. You can think about it, but call me later today, though, and give me an answer," he agreed.

"Okay. I'll call you later today. I've got to go now."

"All right. I'll wait around for your call. I'll stay here; use the same number. I'm at my place. You let me know if you'll have dinner with me."

"Well, when do you want to have this dinner?"

"Tonight would be great!" he almost shouted.

"*Tonight*?"

"Yeah. Tonight would be great. So you'll have dinner with me tonight?"

"I don't know! I told you I'll call you back," I insisted. I had to think and maybe talk to Lydia.

"Okay. I'll wait for your call."

I hung up before he could say more. *Dear God, what could he want? Lord, I can't do this with him any more!* I gathered my things, still sifting through the conversation in my mind. Habit locked the door and drove to Lydia's.

I walked in, greeted the first party arrivals and went directly to the kitchen. Lydia was in the dining room filling the punch bowl.

"There you are!" she smiled when she saw me. "I didn't think you could be lost, but I was beginning to wonder!"

I set the dishes next to the sink and put the sandwiches in the refrigerator.

"I need to talk to you when you get a minute," I told her. I suppose my face had "emergency" written all over it, because she didn't waste any time coming to my side.

"What's going on?" she asked, sliding her hand under my arm in a supportive gesture.

"Jay called," I told her. She stared into my face. "He wants to have dinner."

"What?" Her mouth dropped open and her eyes got wide.

"That's just what I said."

"Sissy! You can't do that! Not after all you've been through with him," she warned.

"Well honey, I don't know what he could possibly want. I don't know what to do."

"You can't meet him. I don't want to see you hurt any more," she begged.

"I'm confused. Why would he call me now? After he got the divorce he wanted?"

"I don't know. I'd be just like you. Why don't you go talk to John? It might be good to have a man's perspective." She ushered me into the living room. John was alone; the kids had congregated in the great room around the food. Lydia left us to attend her guests, and I explained the situation to her husband.

"You're a guy. I need your input here. I just can't figure out what he wants."

"Let me ask you this," he began. "How strong do you feel?"

"That's a good question. I think I'm strong. I know I'm not the person I was when all this mess happened to me three years ago," I mused.

"Well, you pray about it. Ask God to give you a lead, then trust your heart and do what you need to do."

I wound my way through the knot of teenagers in the adjoining room and found Lydia in the kitchen. I told her what John had said.

"Sounds like sage advice to me," she agreed. "Why don't we go in the bedroom and pray about it?"

We checked the food trays and refilled the punch bowl, then retreated into the master suite. We sat on the bed, held hands and prayed. When we'd finished, Lydia hugged me.

"I've got to do the dinner," I told her. "I know it now. Will you be praying for me tonight?"

"You know I will," she assured me. "Just do me one favor. Call me as soon as you get home, okay?" she insisted.

"I'll do that." We took turns at the mirror to repair our tear-streaked faces, then returned to the kids. Most of the guests were gone by 3:00, and I stayed to help Lydia clean up. An hour later, I called Jay.

"Well, I've decided to meet you for dinner," I told him.

"Great!" There was gratitude in his voice.

"How do I dress?"

"Dress up," he told me.

"Where should I meet you?" I wondered what he had in mind.

"No, I don't want you to meet me. Come to my place, and we'll go from here."

I agreed, and he gave me directions. After a couple of missed turns and cell-phone calls for redirection, I found Jay's home. It was a comfortable 32-foot camping trailer parked behind a large office building. After the construction company folded, Jay picked up work where he could. He was now doing maintenance in the building, and the manager had provided him living space. He met me in the yard in a suit and tie.

"Hi Nikki," he said as I got out of the car. "Would you like a cocktail?" he offered, indicating the one he was drinking.

"Sure, I'll have one," I told him, and followed him into the miniature living room. He handed me the drink and we sat on the couch, sipping and chatting about our jobs, working hours, traffic... insignificant trivia to avoid heavier issues. After fifteen minutes, he looked at his watch.

"We've got reservations for eight o'clock," he noted. "I guess we'd better get going."

"I'm ready," I agreed, and followed him to his car.

He drove to one of our favorite haunts, the 42nd Fighter Squadron. The restaurant was situated near a small landing strip and decorated in airplane motif. The smell of old leather and hot steak met us at the door. Jazz floated through the room under a haze of incandescent light. As we were seated, Jay ordered a bottle of wine. He was sparing no expense, I noticed.

The wine and light conversation filled another half-hour. Three times, the waiter came to take our order, but I wasn't ready for food. Finally, my nerves could take no more.

"Look, Jay, all this is nice: the restaurant, the wine, the dressing up and coming to a nostalgic place. But you know, the bottom line is you have something on your mind. I'd just as soon get on with it because first of all, I don't want to have this bottle of wine with you and then drive home. On top of that, I just need to know what you're into here. So let's get down to it: what do you want?"

My mind flashed back to the day he walked in and threw divorce papers in my face two days after I'd had serious surgery. I tried to repress the thought of him and the real estate lady to whom he'd taken a fancy. He set his glass on the table and stared into my eyes. I didn't move.

"I have a question, Nik." He paused, but didn't shift his gaze. "I want to know if we can fix it."

I was glad I had put my glass on the table; I might have choked. "What?" Thinking back on it, I wish I could have seen my face. "Excuse me? You put me through hell for half a dozen years here, and then you have the audacity - I haven't even heard from you in almost a year, other than a check in the mail occasionally - and you just want to know if we can 'fix it?' Oh, this is funny! I'm out of here." I pulled at my purse and shawl and started to get up.

"No, no... please don't go." His eyes were pleading along with his voice. I settled back into position.

"No, I'm telling you there's no chance we can fix it. Where were you when I had cancer surgery? Where were you the night I fell at work and spent nine days flat on my back in pain? What happened to you when I couldn't make my house payments? How dare you just waltz back into my life like nothing happened! You've got a lot of nerve." I could have gone on, but didn't really want to relive the memories.

"I know, I understand. And you're right!" His bright blue eyes were still holding mine.

"Am I right that you got what you wanted? You're a divorced man. So take your darling divorce and put it where the sun don't shine, because it's *over*! Is that clear? It is over." He was quiet for a moment.

"Yeah, that's clear." He rolled his chair around the table and positioned himself right in front of me. I could feel his warm breath as he leaned toward my face, but I didn't move.

"I can imagine how you feel. I was horrible. I treated you rotten. You shouldn't even be talking to me. I am the lowest thing on earth. I understand all that, Nik. I also know what I gave up. I know now what I lost. The only thing I'm gonna ask you is this: is there a possibility for us to fix it? Even if you don't think there is, I think there is. And I'm not gonna let you alone until you give me at least one glimmer of hope! I'm gonna call you, be at your door, hound you. The bottom line is I love you. I want us to fix it; I want to make it up to you. If you can't give me an answer right now, or a possibility of a 'yes,' I will wait around until you do. Period. That's your only option."

As I watched his face, my thoughts focused not on him, but on me. *I can tell you, John Jay, you don't have a chance! Leave me alone. I never want to speak to you again!* But it wasn't what I said.

"All right, here's what I'm gonna do. I will *think* about maybe us *talking* about this, and *if* we talk about the possibility, we're gonna make a list of pros and cons. Then if the pros win, we'll decide what steps we might take to consider it. In the meantime, I'm really hungry. Why don't we go ahead and order dinner, and continue the conversation?"

I don't remember what I ordered. I'd be surprised if three spoonfuls of it ever found their way between my lips. For the next thirty minutes, I shoveled the food around on my plate and tried to look like I was eating. After dinner, we danced to a couple of old favorites, and then it was time to leave.

When we got back to his trailer, we sat on the couch and talked more about his idea to "fix it." I wasn't convinced but was amazed that he was even interested in trying. I got sleepy as we talked and thought I would nap for a few minutes before driving home since it was late, and my house was across town....

The next morning I woke with a blanket over me. The only things amiss were my shoes. Jay had simply covered me and gone to sleep in his own room. It was late in the morning, and he had already left. I was glad to miss rush hour; I was even happier that my shift started at 3 p.m. Before I left for work, I called Lydia.

"Where have you been, girl? I was getting ready to send the cops for you!"

I told her all about the date and about falling asleep. I could hear her sniffling on the other end of the line.

"Sissy, are you okay?" I didn't think my story had been that sappy. She was quiet for a minute, and I knew something was wrong. "Lydia, what is it? What's the matter? Talk to me," I encouraged her.

"Nik, I can't talk about it right now, but I need your prayers. John and I are struggling, and it's getting serious. It's been happening for a while, but I tried to ignore it..." Her voice broke.

"You know I'm praying, honey. I know maybe better than anybody what those kinds of heartaches are about. Do you want me to come over?"

"No, not today. Let's get together soon, though, okay?" she sniffled again and regained her composure.

"You've got it. And you know you can come here any time, don't you?"

"Yeah, I know that, Sissy. Thanks for your prayers."

We hung up the phone, but my heart hung on to my friend. Every thought of her became a prayer.

For the next week, Jay called every day. We talked, but I didn't want to see him. I had too much to think about. I called the counselor at church and made an appointment. For thirty minutes, I told her my feelings about our date and listed all the pros and cons I could think of regarding reconsideration of the relationship.

"What do you think?" I finally asked her.

"Well, Nikki, what do *you* think?" she responded, her words pulling at my heart.

"I still am and probably always will be in love with my husband. But that doesn't mean we can be married to each other. First of all, I'm not even sure where the Lord stands in this marriage, because I'm a Christian, and he's not. He's never going to be a Christian, and I don't want to go back into a marriage that is not founded on the same basis as my life. In other words, if he can't be equally yoked with me, I don't see how our marriage could possibly work out."

"That's a pretty strong statement, Nik. You've come a long way since the last time we talked about this. You have really been healing well, from that person who used to come in here crying and full of guilt to now this woman who can talk logically and face reality. My gosh, you've come full circle! I don't think you have to fear your feelings. You are very capable of making strong decisions. Either way you go, I think you're going to make good ones. Just continue to keep Christ first in this process, as you have been. I think your vacillation is because you don't want to hurt Jay if your decisions aren't in his favor. Think about that. Don't be hasty, just continue like you're going. You're doing fine."

Her words gave me confidence. I knew God had been growing me, changing me, preparing me to make good decisions. I talked to Him constantly, even with my eyes wide open, carrying on daily activities. I knew my relationship with Him was first, regardless of what would happen with Jay. I was no longer depending on a man to meet my needs; I had learned that the Lord is the only one who is perfect, and He is the only one who deserves to control my life and decision-making. What would happen between Jay and me was in God's hands.

Two weeks after our initial meeting, he called and asked for a second dinner date. This one was to be casual, and he wanted me to come to his place again and go from there. I was sitting in his living room waiting when he came out of the bedroom with his hands behind his back. He sat down on the couch and extended a little fuzzy box in my direction.

"Oh, no," I said. "I don't want whatever you have in that box."

"You don't even know what's in the box. It could be a marble, for all you know!" he teased.

"It doesn't matter, Jay. Listen to me: I don't want what's in the box!"

"Well, open it anyway."

I took it from him and opened the lid. There inside was my original engagement ring. After the divorce, I had virtually destroyed it when I'd asked a neighbor to cut it from my finger with his hedge shears. I'd returned it to Jay, mangled just like our marriage. Here it was, perfectly restored and ready to wear. I closed the box and handed it back to him. His face fell, and he stared at the floor.

"Why are you doing this?" he asked me quietly.

"Jay, you need to understand something. First of all, I haven't told you we're gonna fix this. Just because we are going on a second date doesn't give you a foot in. Don't even think it! This may not go the way you think it should. I want to assure you that however it goes, it's going to be right for both of us. In the meantime, let's just go to dinner and have fun."

He put the box on the side table and looked at me.

"Okay," he said. "Fair enough."

We went out, ate dinner and went dancing. It was great fun. Throughout that summer, we spent lots of time together seeing movies, cooking out on his deck, preparing meals at my place. It was a comfortable, good friendship. We were both happy with that; I was making certain the relationship didn't move to a romantic or sexual one. I was observing him, mentally noting attitudes and responses. One night while we were sitting on his deck our conversation went again to the possibility of a future together.

"You know, Jay, you've got all these ideas in your mind about how it's going to be. You don't know me. You really don't. I'm not the person you left. I'm not that girl that would get knocked down drunk and party and fight with you. I'm not her anymore. My plans for my future are not like they were. I don't think the same way. I don't go to the places I used to frequent. I'm just not her. You wouldn't like me anymore. Right now you might think you like me. You even think you love me, but you really don't. I could get on your nerves the way I am now."

I knew he wouldn't understand if I told him a Christian and a non-believer couldn't necessarily be a compatible match. In a kind way, I think I was trying to run him off. In my heart, this time we were spending together was becoming closure, and I was content with it. I didn't want to give him false hope. At the same time, I was growing in my respect for him, and the love I had in my heart had never changed.

It was toward the end of the summer when he came out of the bedroom again with the little fuzzy box.

"Nik," he said, sitting down beside me, "I really want you to wear this. I would like to think we have some hope for fixing our life together in the future if you'd wear this ring."

My heart surprised me with a definite answer. I know now that the Holy Spirit often uses quiet impressions to whisper God's will. He said, *You have to do this.* I received the box and sat holding it for a moment.

"I'll tell you what. How about if I wear the ring with this in mind: if you will promise me that as a couple, we can do counseling for one year. At the end of that time, we can make a decision as to where we think we are and what the next step should be."

He considered that suggestion.

"That is so much more than I could ever have imagined. Yeah, Nik. We can do that. Why don't you choose the counselor and set it up. I'll do whatever you need me to do."

"You promise?" I was going to hold him to his word.

"I promise," he smiled as he answered. He took the ring from its rest and placed it on my finger. We had a conditional engagement.

"You know, Jay, after counseling, you or me or both of us may decide this isn't really where we want to be. Maybe we'll realize we've outgrown each other, and it's better if we go our separate ways. Right now, I think we need a cooling off period. We need to take a closer look and not rush this; there's no reason to hurry!"

"Hey - I'm happy to do this. You set it up, and I'll do it."

I came right home and called the church for an appointment. After my counselor heard what we'd said and what I told him, I asked her what she thought about it.

"I think you already know what you need to do, and you've done a great job!" she assured me. "You should be so proud of yourself. Look at the pressure you were under, how tempted you must have been... the doubts and fears you've had. I'm excited to be a part of this. By all means, go and set it up!"

I arranged with her receptionist for monthly appointments.

By the end of the summer, we were in counseling. At least once a month for an hour or more, we talked through our issues and dug into the drudge that had come between us in the past. One Saturday evening as we enjoyed a September sunset, Jay became serious.

"You know, you've never even invited me to your church."

"Yes, I have!" I countered, remembering mentioning to him while we were still separated that I was attending a church.

"That was before. I mean since we've been seeing each other this summer. Why don't you invite me again?"

I had avoided discussing church or my faith with him; I didn't want him to come to services with me thinking he would use spirituality as an inroad into my heart. He'd never seen a need for religion, and I didn't think he was serious. If he wanted to seek the Lord, he was going to do it without persuasion from me.

"Well, okay then," I said without enthusiasm. "Come to church with me sometime."

"Yeah! Great. How about tomorrow?"

I turned to look at his face. Was he kidding?

"All right. That will be fine. Really?"

"Yeah, really."

"Okay." I doubted he would follow through, but I was happy he'd brought it up. Later as we were preparing to go out to dinner, I reminded him. It was a test of sorts, to see how committed he was to going with me.

"If you're going with me tomorrow," I said, "the church is much closer to my house than to yours; why don't you grab a change of clothes and stay at my house tonight? Then in the morning we can go together."

To my amazement, he agreed and gathered his things.

The Praise Team already knew that Jay and I had been seeing the counselor, and they were excited to meet him the next day. Everyone who knew me treated him like a celebrity, and he also enjoyed the worship service. After that first Sunday, he started coming every week. He loved the pastor and sometimes would talk to me about his messages. Soon after that first encounter, he requested to join the tech team to help in the sound booth, and they welcomed him with open arms.

Like individuals, churches make mistakes. Our congregation and leadership made one when my healing was not publicized. In that instance, we missed an opportunity to offer God glory. However, when Jay came, the love of Christ glowed through His children and drew him to Jesus' side. It was a joy for me to watch believers in our congregation accepting and encouraging Jay, and to see him responding to the God he saw in them.

The following week, I was at his trailer one afternoon when he got a mischievous look in his eyes.

"I want to show you something," he said, smiling.

"Okay... What is it?" He had my curiosity peaked already.

"It's a surprise. Come on. We'll go in the truck."

We jumped in and he drove around the block to a warehouse. The building was a simple concrete structure with loading docks along one three hundred-foot side wall and a walk-in entrance on the front. Jay parked and used a key to open the door. I followed him through a musty office and down a dim hallway to another interior door. When we opened it, all I could see was an expanse of room. It was bigger than a gymnasium, but it seemed to be empty.

"What is this about?" I asked him, still clueless.

"Just follow me," he answered, walking toward the far end of the building. As we approached, I could see something stacked against the wall. Moving closer, I noticed cardboard cartons, about four inches square and several feet long, stacked from the floor to the ceiling across the entire width of the building.

"What is this?" I questioned, still standing at a distance.

"Go up there and have a look," Jay said, crossing his arms and wearing a smug grin.

I walked closer and my mouth dropped open.

"Well, what do you think?" he pressed.

"Why, you.... I'm just blown away. I can't believe you finally did it. You stinker! You rat!" I teased him, smiling now myself. "How did you... Who produced... These are the thing-a-ma-bobs, aren't they?"

"Yep. We call them 'slide bobs' now." He joined me at the base of the stack. "Do you recognize the guy on the picture?"

For a moment, I was speechless.

"Home Depot is getting ready to send these into test markets in several states. This is just the first batch," he told me with proud assurance.

"I'm so surprised! Shocked might be a better word. All this time, and you didn't even tell me?"

Jay took my hand, and I turned to face him.

"I wanted to be sure that if you were ever willing to marry me, it would be for me, and not for what I might have," he answered quietly.

"You should know I'd never marry you anyway if I didn't love you!" I told him. "I am really proud of you."

Every autumn, the men of the church have a weekend retreat. When I knew the time was approaching, I mentioned it to Jay.

"Would you like to go?"

"I'll think about it," was all he would tell me. The next week, I asked him if he'd made a decision, but he was still noncommittal.

"Is it just that you don't *want* to go?" I asked him, trying to understand his hesitancy.

"Not really," he admitted. "It's quite expensive, and I don't think I can afford it right now," he said.

I understood, and dropped the subject, but I couldn't get it off my mind. I thought it would be good if he could spend some time with Christian men and get to know them outside the context of the church. If it was money and not a lack of desire holding him back, perhaps that could be remedied. On Wednesday, I called the office.

"Hello. May I help you?" the receptionist answered.

We chatted casually for a moment. "Actually, I called because I was wondering who I might talk to about the men's retreat," I explained to her.

"I hate to tell you this, dear, but you don't qualify."

We both laughed.

"Seriously, what would you like to know?"

"Well, Jay is considering going to the retreat, but there may be a financial hindrance. I thought maybe I could help pay his way," I told her.

"I think there may be some scholarship money available for these kinds of situations," she said. She found the name of a contact person.

"This is wonderful! I will call him and ask about it. Thanks so much!"

When I told Jay what I'd done, and that there was scholarship money available, at first he was a little embarrassed that I had called. Later though, when the guys on the tech team kept asking him about it, he decided to go.

I was in his kitchen preparing a hot meal when he got home that Sunday night. I had just washed my hands and sat down on the deck in a lawn chair when he drove up. He hurried out of the car and bounded up the steps wearing a broad smile.

"Looks like somebody had a good time," I smiled back, rising to give him a hug.

"Guess what?"

"I can't imagine," I said, waiting for a story.

"I gave my life to God. I'm a new Christian!"

Chapter Eighteen

What the Locusts Had Eaten

We danced around the deck clinging to each other and crying. It was a gift I never expected. However, I still was not ready to promise him anything. We continued with our counseling sessions. I was working hard to rebuild my trust in him, praying and hoping he was indeed serious and not playing some kind of wicked game. Once in a while he'd ask me if I was ready to set a date, and I would put him off.

Even before the retreat, Jay had started attending Christian small group meetings with me. Now he wanted us to study the Bible together. Five months after the retreat, I knew in my heart God was at work in Jay's life, and that He had indeed brought us together to keep us that way. In February, we discussed our thoughts with the counselor.

"Maybe if things continue to progress, we can think in terms of a summer wedding," I suggested.

"I think that will work. You have fulfilled your obligations to one another regarding these sessions," she said. "I think you could build a Christian marriage."

That was the turning point in our relationship. We were now serious rather than conditional about our engagement.

After Valentine's Day, I started making wedding plans. We decided to get married on June 5th, and the pastor agreed to sign our certificate on the 6th, our original anniversary. That was the first of many blessings around this wedding; some were nothing short of miraculous.

The first of the miracles was the response of my brother, Chuck. Ever since my conversion, I had gently tried to talk to him about a personal relationship with God, but he was not convinced. He clung to his atheistic stance. At first when I spoke with him about participating in the wedding, he was sure he couldn't come. However, within the week, his conflict dissolved, and he was able to be part of our ceremony. I considered that a miracle.

One catalyst for several other miracles was a special song that God brought to my attention. I was in the car on my way to the restaurant where we were planning to have the reception. A Christian radio station was playing a piece I'd never heard by Nicole C. Mullen.

"I know my Redeemer lives," she sang. Tears spilled down my cheeks and clouded my vision. As I listened further, I had to pull off the road. I found myself weeping for joy and praising God, sitting in my car in a deserted parking lot. For some reason, the words pricked my soul, and I thought about singing it at the wedding. *A bride doesn't sing at her own wedding,* my heart objected. But the Holy Spirit kept prompting me, so on the way home that day, I stopped and bought the *Redeemer* CD. Every time I listened to the song, it broke me.

I had asked a friend from the worship team, Kim, to sing another song for the ceremony, so I assumed at the time she would also sing "Redeemer." But as I thought and prayed about the event, I became convinced God wanted me to do it. I took the CD home and started memorizing.

In the meantime, all of the arrangements were being made. Alterations to the dress I'd worn when Jay and I married the first time allowed me to use it again, after over a decade – no small miracle in itself. All three of my children and their families would be here and one of Jay's girls as well! Just as all the details were falling into place, disaster struck.

I only lacked three months having my car paid off, but Murphy's law went into full swing a week and a half before the wedding. As I was driving, the car suddenly lost power and wouldn't pick up speed. In the middle of Duluth's weekend traffic, I found myself in the center lane, flooring the accelerator and moving at fifteen miles per hour. I was terrified, but didn't panic. I put on the flashers, eased the car to the edge of the street, and called Jay.

"Honey, I don't know what's going on, but I'm stuck here with a crippled car. Can you come?"

"What happened?" he wanted to know.

I explained the strange loss of power.

"Sounds like the generator," he said. "That's not good. Listen, lock the car and go wait in a building somewhere. I'll call you again when I get close."

Within the hour, my hero had arrived, tools in hand. He tinkered with my sick engine for more than a half-hour, then decided we should take it to a mechanic.

"I'll follow you in my truck," he said. "That way, if it quits in the road and there are no tail lights, no one else will rear end you. I think there's a station with a shop down about two miles..." He gave me detailed directions, and we agreed to stay in touch on our cell phones.

Twenty minutes later we had made it the two miles and located the repair place. Jay explained the car's behavior, and the mechanic changed some parts, installed hoses and belts, and made other adjustments while we waited. Four hundred eighty-five dollars later, the problem still wasn't fixed. We headed for home, but ten miles down the road, the same symptoms occurred again and the car lost power. I couldn't encourage it in any way to pick up speed.

We stopped at a junkyard on the way, and Jay talked to the manager.

"No, this car's too new. We don't have parts that would fit that model," he apologized.

"Do you have any idea what could be wrong?"

"Nope. If the mechanic checked the generator and said it was okay, I am without a clue." It took us two hours to finally make it back to Woodstock.

"What am I gonna do?" I asked him when we got in the house. "I can't function without a car. I've got to get to work!"

"I know," he replied, picking up the newspaper and unfolding the ads section. "We're gonna find you another car."

"I don't think buying someone's used junk is really a good option this time," I told him. "Wonder what a down payment costs? What we have left might make one."

He looked up and studied my face.

"Why don't we go find out?"

We shopped at four car dealerships before finding the one we wanted and could afford. When the day was over, I had a new car, but the money had come from funds that were designated for the reception arrangements. The club required complete payment in advance.

"What am I gonna tell Cathy?" I said to Jay.

"Ask her if we can make payments for the balance," he suggested.

It sounded like a workable plan, but I was still a bit embarrassed to have to call her and request a change of arrangements.

"Hello," said a familiar voice.

"Cathy? This is Nikki. I hope you're having a good day," I started.

"Yes, so far. What can I do for you? I guess you're getting excited with the wedding a little over a week away."

"Yeah, something like that. Listen, I need to let you know that this morning we had a car emergency, and I'm not going to be able to finish paying the balance on our account before the wedding. I know that's your policy, and I am really in a bad place; I don't know what to do. The invitations have been out for weeks, and my family will be arriving in just a few days–"

She interrupted me.

"You know that's our policy. I'm afraid I can't continue the arrangements without all the money. There is no way I can help you. You will either have to come up with the balance or find yourself another venue. My bosses won't allow me to do a reception on credit. If you have another plan, you let me know, but we've only got a short amount of time in which to do this. I'm surprised you'd call me at this point and announce you can't pay!"

Her words were edgy, and I could tell she was angry.

"I can assure you I didn't plan to run out of money. We had it set aside, but my car just died in the road! I still have to get to work; I can't live without a car. Listen, I'll try to think of something. Please don't be angry with me; it really was unavoidable."

"Just call me if you come up with a plan. I already have quite a bit of stuff on order, and I need to hear from you soon."

"Okay. Thank– "

She had hung up. What could I do? How could I have a wedding without a reception? How could I ask my friends to celebrate with us and then not give them a place to do it? *Father, only You can fix this. She has a right to be angry; I signed a contract! She*

*could sue me. You've certainly done harder things. I
know you are concerned about details as well as big
stuff. So here's a detail. Help, please!*

I was in the car on the way to the grocery store
three hours later when my cell phone rang. I fished it
from its case, trying to keep one eye on the road.

"Hello."

"Hello, Nikki? This is Cathy."

"Hi Cathy," I returned, bracing myself for her to
tell me she'd have to cancel the whole thing.

"Nikki, can you come by my office? I've been
thinking about your situation, and I'm sorry I got
so angry. It's just that I have to answer for all these
things when they don't go right. It's my responsibility, and my boss will get mad at me. I shouldn't
have taken it out on you. It kind of hit me cold, and I
reacted out of fear," she explained.

"I completely understand your anger," I told her.
"I'm sure in your position I would feel the same way.
After all, I'm asking you to change the contract I've
already signed. I'm just not sure where to go from
here."

"That's why I asked if you can come by my office.
I have a plan. Why don't we sit down and see how
we can shave some things off, shuffle some items
around and reduce the price? I do want you to have a
wonderful wedding. What's going on in your life is
so unusual, so rare. I just want to help if I can. Maybe
we can rearrange some things and still come up with
a really nice celebration for you."

I could taste tears of joy in my throat. "Oh my gosh... If you'd be willing to do that, it would mean so much to me."

"Can you come tomorrow morning?" she asked.

We decided on ten o'clock. *Thank You, Father, for Your answer.* I smiled as tears dribbled over my cheeks.

The next morning, we sat together looking at the things she'd suggested, trimming some details and cutting a few corners. In less than an hour, we came up with a workable solution.

"Now you owe me twenty dollars," Cathy announced with a smile.

"That's sure better than fifteen hundred!" I laughed. I paid her the twenty and she gave me a hug.

"No one will ever miss the things we omitted," she said. I knew she was right. It would still be a fabulous evening. It was another miracle for which I could praise my Father.

Two days later, with only six left before the wedding, I had been practicing on the song I was to sing when my throat started feeling scratchy. The next morning, I woke with a full-blown cold and sinus infection. I couldn't speak above a whisper and didn't dare try to sing! I gargled with salt water, sprayed my throat with medicine, rested my voice... I tried every homespun remedy anyone suggested, but three days before the wedding, I was still barking and sniffling. My voice sounded two octaves lower and was quite congested. I called Kim.

"You'd better learn the words to 'Redeemer,' I told her. "I don't think I'm going to be able to do it."

Friday night came and with it, the rehearsal. Our pastor preached from Joel, and at the end of the ceremony, I had Kim sing my song. Lydia was my maid of honor. She came to me before the dinner. I knew that she and John were having some serious problems, and that divorce was being considered. They were constantly in my thoughts and prayers.

"Nikki," she said, touching my arm. I turned and saw her tear-streaked face. "I know that sermon is for John and me. I couldn't stop weeping! God is gonna restore us," she said. It was a beginning.

The next afternoon, the ceremony got off to a late start. I went into a classroom outside the sanctuary to finish my preparations. Kim came in and closed the door.

"Nikki, what about the song? Are you going to sing it, or do you want me to?"

I was sitting in a chair, staring at her. I knew God had given me that song and when He did, He told me to sing it. But I hadn't practiced all week! My voice had been cracking and pitiful even today. How could I sing the song? How could I *not* sing the song! *Well, fine then! Here's the throat, Lord, and here's the voice. It's Your miracle!*

"Kim, I'm gonna sing the song," I croaked. She smiled.

"All right! That's the spirit," she said, leaning over to hug me. She left the room, and the entire wedding party followed her.

Dad walked me down the aisle where my groom was waiting. The pastor, who had recently resigned his position, looked at us, then at the congregation seated behind us.

"This is a kind of culmination of my entire ministry in this church," he said. "To see in these two people what God can do." He prayed and we did our vows, then Kim sang her song. Afterward, the pastor stood again to give his message.

"In the book of Joel, we find these words:

I will repay you for the years the locusts have eaten – the great locust and the young locust, the other locusts and the locust swarm – my great army that I sent among you. You will have plenty to eat, until you are full, and you will praise the name of the Lord your God, who has worked wonders for you..."

Our pastor friend couldn't have known just how many wonders God had worked for us, nor how many were yet to be done among His children gathered in that place. When he had finished his sermon, I turned to face the congregation and the music began. After the introduction, I opened my mouth to sing, and the words flowed! No cracks, no breaks, no uncertainty. I lifted my hands and sang from my heart: "I know my Redeemer lives!" My eyes panned the congregation. I saw Jay's daughter standing near the front, her face tear-streaked and smiling. Her dad had already shared his faith with her, and now she was seeking the Lord. To one side stood my brother, watching me intently. Then my eyes found Lydia's John, sitting with the other groomsmen. Tears streamed down his face. *Lord, use Your song to let them know You live, and You love them so much! So many in this group need miracles...*

The song was over, and I hadn't missed a note! God had touched people. He had made me weak so that He could show off again through my life.

"Nikki!" Kim said as soon as we got into the foyer. "How did you do that? Every time we rehearsed, you couldn't even get the words out! The whole time you were singing, I had chills all over me. You were witnessing for Christ. And you know what? The more you sang, the stronger your voice got!"

Jay and I stood side by side in the receiving line. The impossible had happened already, but God wasn't finished. As my brother came through the line, he hugged me.

"Sis, I just want you to know something," he said looking me straight in the eye. "I believed every word that you said, and I am talking to God."

"WHAT?" I said, smiling and hugging him again.

"Yes, I am," he repeated.

As he walked on down the line, I chalked that one up as another of God's miracles. Several others greeted us. John was not with Lydia early in the procession but came later with the other groomsmen. He clung to me for a moment as we hugged, speaking into my ear.

"I have been so blessed, Nikki. My eyes have opened today. I can't tell you how much I appreciate it. You have no idea the difference this whole thing has made in my life. I see miracles here," he said as he moved toward Jay.

"John, that is wonderful, honey. We love you so much, and you guys are gonna be fine. I believe that in my heart," I told him.

During the reception, John and Lydia danced together. She told me later what she said as she leaned on his shoulder.

"I'm believing this for us," she whispered.

She had seen God restore what the locusts had eaten. And she knew He could do it again. Maybe someday, she will tell you her story.

Issues for Thought and Discussion

Chapter 1
1. Where is God when a child is molested?
    a. Exodus 22:22 –
        - How are abused children like orphans?
        - What is God's stand toward them according to this verse?
    b. Ephesians 6:4 –
        - What happens inside a child when their caregivers betray them?
        - What is God's counsel about this?
    c. Colossians 3:21 –
        - What warning is God giving here for parents?
        - How is a child's soul crushed by abuse?

2. What should parents teach children regarding their bodies and boundaries?
3. How did Nikki's grandparents' relationship shape her definition of marriage?
4. What memories do you have from preschool age regarding:
    a. Parents' relationship
    b. Home environment
    c. People outside your immediate family
5. What values, habits or opinions do you still carry today as a result of those influences?

Chapter 2
1. List reasons for Nikki's feelings of betrayal and abandonment.
2. How did Nikki try to solve her problem?
3. Have you ever felt betrayed or abandoned? How did you deal with the pain?
4. List three promises God makes to those in Nikki's situation.
    a. John 14:27 –
    b. Matthew 28:20b –
    c. 1 John 4:4 –
    d. Other promises –

Chapter 3
1. What had Nikki learned about people by the time she was fifteen? List as many items as possible.
2. Who did Nikki turn to for deliverance from her situation?

3. What was the basis for Bert's attractions to Nikki? For hers to him?
4. Describe Biblical love (see 1 Corinthians 13). On what were Nikki and Bert building their relationship?

Chapter 4
1. In what, at the beginning of the chapter, is Nikki basing her personal fulfillment?
2. List four methods God used in this chapter to warn, protect or nurture Nikki.
3. What circumstances or people has God used in your life to communicate His love, care and protection to you? (1 John 3:11)

Chapter 5
1. What factors came together in Nikki's life to push her to attempt suicide?
2. Which of Nikki's choices in this chapter directly impacted her children?
3. How did bitterness about her mother and Tony impact Nikki's own life and decision-making?
4. Is there bitterness in your soul about something? How is it impacting you? How is it impacting those around you? (Hebrews 12:15)

Chapter 6
1. List the avenues Nikki took to deal with her emotional pain.

2. In what ways was Nikki a "good mother" during those years of addiction?
3. In light of the incident of Coppertone's death, what was Nikki's biggest problem with parenting during those years? On whom was her primary focus?
4. How is God's love different from human love? How can His love change one's focus?

Chapter 7
1. What did Spectrum Programs provide Nikki by stripping away and gradually rebuilding her personal responsibilities?
2. List things in your life that require boundaries. Example: time I will spend with others, my budget, my food and substance intake, etc.
3. How does the Lordship of Christ redefine the boundaries of one's life? (Galatians 5:1)

Chapter 8
1. List some good results and bad consequences of choices Nikki had made to this point.
2. Have you ever been judged unjustly for something in your past? How did you feel about that?
3. Is there anyone in your life you need to forgive in order to clear bitterness from your own heart? (Ephesians 4:31-32)

Chapter 9
1. What do you think Nikki was searching for that she thought she'd found in Renzo?
2. On what assumptions had Nikki based her relationship with Renzo?
3. What were Renzo's expectations of Nikki?
4. Why did Nikki finally confront Renzo?
5. List red flags in their relationship. On what should a healthy relationship be based? (Ephesians 4:25, 29)

Chapter 10
1. Describe what initially attracted Nikki to Fred. What needs in her life was she subconsciously trying to meet?
2. What was Fred like? What problems in his personality compounded the difficulties in his marriage to Nikki?
3. List strengths this chapter reveals in Nikki's character. How is strength of character different from peace of mind? (John 10:10, John 14:1)

Chapter 11
1. How does alcoholism destroy families? On what is an alcoholic dependent? Why?
2. What created an emotional bond between Nikki and Jay?
3. What steps of bonding do you believe are needed for a healthy marriage, and in what order? (Genesis 2:24 – three steps)

4. What do you think Nikki expected from her relationship with Jay?

Chapter 12
1. Note the issues that became more important than money in this chapter:
    a. For Nikki and Jay –
    b. For Johnny Dollar –
2. List four things you would change about your life if you learned today you had inoperable cancer.
3. How can you attain lasting inner peace? (John 14:27, Ps. 29:11, Is. 26:3)

Chapter 13
1. Why did Nikki become disillusioned with the music business?
2. Have you ever had to bury a dream? What impact has that disappointment made in your own life?
3. How would you respond if one of your children contracted a serious illness through promiscuity or homosexual activity? (Gal. 6:1-2)

Chapter 14
1. Why did Nikki initially respond the way she did to Em's death?
2. How can you offer comfort when a friend loses a son or daughter in death?
3. See John 11:33. The Greek notes that Jesus was moved with *indignation*. Why do you

think he was indignant (angry)? How is that
Scripture a comfort for grieving people?

Chapter 15
1. Have you ever had a near-death experience?
   If so, what did you learn from it?
2. As Jay's business grew and became more
   lucrative, what slipped through the cracks?
3. Name four intentional things that can keep
   a marriage between two very busy people
   together.
4. What had made Lydia approachable since
   the last time Nikki had spent time with her?
5. How does God use pain in our lives?
   (2 Corinthians 1:4)

Chapter 16
1. What important lessons did God teach Nikki
   through Tom?
2. List two unlikely sources through which
   God has taught you key lessons.
3. How has her pattern of dependence changed
   since Nikki asked Christ to take over her
   life?
4. Who do you depend on for security? What
   evidence proves this is true?

Chapter 17
1. At the beginning of the chapter, how did
   Nikki make her decision to meet Jay for
   dinner? Why is godly counsel important in

a Christian's life? (Jer. 17:9, Prov. 1:7, Prov. 15:22)
2. Why was Nikki hesitant to rekindle her relationship with Jay? (2 Cor. 6:14)
3. How had Nikki's priorities changed?
4. Why was courtship necessary again? What bonds needed rebuilding?
5. How can you be intentional in strengthening your marriage or your most important friendships?

Chapter 18
1. Why did Jay's newfound faith in Christ change Nikki's attitude toward their relationship?
2. How did Nikki and Jay's remarriage impact others in their family circle?
3. How does your faith impact your extended family?
4. How does your marriage express your faith?
5. What would you like to change about your marriage in order to more clearly demonstrate God's glory?
6. Consider how God has worked miraculously in your own life. Offer Him praise.

Printed in the United States
91166LV00001B/10-15/A